Malice, Murder, and Manipulation

One man's quest for truth

by

Grant Arthur Gochin

DEDICATION

To the joy of my life, my son, Bryce Gochin-Lyon.

The darkest places in hell are reserved for those who maintain their neutrality in times of moral crisis. —Dante Alighieri

Justice, justice shall you pursue, —Deuteronomy 16:20

Our dead are never dead to us, until we have forgotten them.—George Eliot

ACKNOWLEDGEMENTS

With gratitude to my beloved husband, Russell Lyon, for his patience.

To my mothers, Sandra Gochin and Valerie Smollan, for their constant love and support.

To all those who assisted along the way, THANK YOU. Some of the many to whom I extend my gratitude are Egle Bendikaite, Sergey Kanovich, Marylin Kingston, and Darius Udrys.

To my beloved grandfather Samuel Gochin, thank you for the gift of heritage, the stories, and the love.

To my grandmother Bee Smollan, born Brocha Leya Novosedz, daughter of Sire Elke Garrenbloom and Iankel Ber Novosedz, in Birzai, Lithuania, thank you for the Litvak concepts of human dignity. A greater teacher never existed.

GRANT ARTHUR GOCHIN

TABLE OF CONTENTS

MALICE, MURDER, AND MANIPULATION

GENEALOGY

<u>Father to son</u>

Faiva

Avram (married Chaie)

Sam (siblings were Freyda, Dora, Tsipa, Edel, Jack, and Esther)

Harold

Grant

TIMELINE

1837	Faive born
11/13/1866	Avram born
1/20/1874	Chaie born
2/15/1902	Sam born

1913   FAMILY PHOTOGRAPH

7/28/1914	WWI begins
02/1915	Sam's bar mitzvah
4/17/1915	Saiuliai vital records destroyed
5/4/1915	Jews deported from Papile
1917	Sam abducted into the Byelorussian military
2/16/1918	Lithuania declared independent
11/11/1918	WWI ends
1/9/1919	New Lithuanian government seated

7/12/1920	Soviet-Lithuanian Peace Treaty signed
10/20/1921	Mones returns from deportation
12/21/1921	Papile Jewish community issues replacement birth records
12/26/1921	Faive Gochin applies for permission for the return of the family
2/5/1922	Jakob Scala dies of TB
2/9/1922	Avram dies of starvation
2/9/1922	Edel dies of starvation
2/28/1922	Council of Papile gives testimony
3/28/1922	Lithuanian Department of Citizens Security issues denial
4/4/1922	Gershon Ioffe and both children die of starvation
4/13/1922	Freyda dies of pneumonia
4/18/1922	Denial issued to Faiva
6/6/1922	Tsipa dies of typhoid
9/27/1922	Chaie crosses into Lithuania
1923	Sam returns to Lithuania
4/10/1923	Internal passport issued to Chaie
1924	Independent Lithuanian Army begins operation
1924	Sam conscripted into Lithuanian Army

6/6/1924	Sam admitted to military hospital
11/5/1924	Sam & Esther issued Lithuanian internal passports
1925	Sam released from Lithuanian military service
1/15/1926	Sam re-issued internal passport
02/1926	Sam departs for South Africa
3/22/1926	Faive dies
3/25/1926	Sam arrives in Port Elizabeth, South Africa
12/26/1929	Sam is married
04/1930	Chaie and Esther arrive in South Africa
7/28/1931	Sam is naturalized as a South African citizen
6/13/1933	Harold born
6/23–8/5/1941	Lithuanian Activist Front governs Lithuania

07/1941	Jews of Papile moved into ghettos
8/22/1941	Noreika signs orders
10/2/1941	Most Jews of Papile are murdered
1943	Mones and his family are murdered
5/22/1949	Chaie dies
11/2/1963	Grant born
6/2/1984	Sam dies
3/11/1990	Lithuania regains independence
1995	Skirpa re-burial in Lithuania
12/31/2004	Grant applies for Lithuanian citizenship
6/18/2007	Citizenship denied
2/25/2008	First court decision
9/18/2008	Second court decision
6/22/2009	Grant applies for Right of Retention
1/21/2010	Right of Retention denied
9/23/2010	Third court decision
2010	School named in honor of Noreika
6/22/2011	Restitution is settled
7/21/2011	Fourth case—Lithuania's Supreme Administrative Court rules
10/26/2011	Right of Retention issued
05/2012	LAF Prime Minister Brazaitis re-buried with State Honors in Lithuania

PREFACE

I grew up learning about the "old country," which in my home meant Lithuania; my paternal grandfather often regaled me with stories of the old country. It became inseparable from my Jewishness.

My Jewishness was taught as a code of conduct rather than a religious belief. It was about the upliftment of humanity, human dignity, education, and personal improvement.

Every family has its own story, and this story is a genealogical study of my family—and how legal citizenship dramatically affected their lives. It is a story of murder, injustice, criminality, and finally, a miniscule modicum of accountability.

This book is written to memorialize the suffering of those who went before, so our younger generation may learn what happened, how it enabled us to live the lives we have today, and how very few of our families survived to enjoy life. May our youth realize that even the most privileged amongst us suffered absolute horrors just a few short years ago. May they learn the randomness of survival and the appreciation owed to our common forebears.

An asset those few survivors inadvertently passed forward is possible citizenship rights to their place of prior geography. These are rights, no different than any other right—we just need to claim them, and in doing so, preserve the memory of our ancestors and our current and future legal rights.

The voices of our ancestors have been silenced through murder and victimization. By writing this story, we give voice to one family, and by extrapolation, to many more. We preserve their lives and memory, and thus honor them. L'Dor V'Dor.

PART I

We travel on a journey through time. Some survived, most did not. Jewish migration and Jewish citizenship rights affected life and death, and the very survival of Jews in Europe. We are the tattered remnants, tasked with memory. This book is about memory.

In 1913, the Gochin family of Papile, of the Siauliai District of Lithuania, sat for a family photograph. Of the seven Gochin children, only Freida Leya was absent.

Lithuanian records show that Gochins had lived in Papile since the late 1700s. Prior documents do not exist. Probably this family had lived in Lithuania for 700 years, the extent of Jewish presence in the land of the Lithuanian Empire.

c. 1913

HISTORY

World War I broke out on July 28, 1914. Battle lines spread to present-day Lithuania.

On April 17, 1915, Germans troops descended on Siauliai from several directions. Russian troops deliberately burned the city, torching 800 houses, including the home of the state rabbi, together with his archives and Jewish vital records, and also the city offices and city archives. Most of houses that burned belonged to Jews[1].

Russia, a deeply anti-Semitic nation, viewed Jews as a potential threat; and since Jews were a convenient minority target on which Russians focused their wrath for losing their war, they blamed Jews for their losses. Nikolai Nikolaevich, the Russian Tzar's uncle, was required to explain Russian defeats, and so he accused all Jews of being German spies, and ordered their expulsion. Vast numbers of Jews were deported into the Russian hinterlands. Approximately 150,000 Jews were deported from the Kaunas region alone.

Local district officials carrying out the deportation orders performed their duties with maximum cruelty—most orders were effected within 24 hours of issuance, no matter the age or health status of the victim. Reports from Pasvalys Jews stated that they were packed into cattle cars for ten days of transportation without the wagons being opened a single time.[2] During and after expulsions and evacuations, local Lithuanians plundered the property of the expellees, without intervention from local authorities.

On May 4, 1915, the Jewish family Gochin, in a small village called Papile, in the Siauliai District in Northern Lithuania, was one of

---

[1]

http://www.eilatgordinlevitan.com/siauliai/siau_pages/siauliai_stories_1915.html

[2]Fourth Duma (Note 56), p. 443, from speech delivered by V.I. Dziubinskii.

thousands of families deported. The family was deported to Melitopol in Ukraine.

These now dispossessed Jews were forbidden from living in the countryside, and farming was not allowed. After the 1917 Russian Revolution, trading in grain was disallowed for all peoples, and therefore Jews and others starved and died in massive numbers. Given that these Jewish deportees were not native to the lands of their deportations, without family networks, they suffered and died disproportionately.

Jewish deaths and suffering from 1915–1923 were overshadowed by the later Holocaust, and are therefore hardly recorded in our history books.

From hearings in front of the U.S. Committee on Immigration and Naturalization, in the House of Representatives, in the 64th Congress, first session on H.R. 558 on Thursday, January 20, 1916, concerning restriction of immigration into the United States, testimony showed that hundreds of thousands of Jews had been wantonly deported from the Provinces of Grodno, Kovno, and Kurland in Eastern Europe. Facts presented to the U.S. Congress were compiled exclusively from Russian newspapers, which had already passed the scrutiny of the Russian

Military Censors.[3]

The Polish newspaper, *Ziemia Lubelska*, in its edition #111 of April 23, 1915, reported: "In the region where the Jews constituted over 80 percent of the total population of the small towns, at present not a single Jew is to be found in those same towns situated in the zone of Military operations."

The first Jewish expulsion in Lithuania came in March 1915, in the village Botki, near Taurage, blamed on false accusations of Jews poisoning the town well in order to poison Christian Lithuanians. (If that were so, what water would the Jews have drunk?)

In the latter part of April and in early May of 1915, expulsion of the Jews was ordered on an enormous scale extending over the provinces of Grodno, Kovno, and Kurland. In order that the expelled residents of Kovno would never be able to return to their homes, the Administration ordered all Jews to be struck from the Registration Books, as no longer legally residing within the zone of the Kovno Fortress.

Jews were deported with sometimes a few hours' notice, other times a day or two. They were unable to take food provisions, sanitary provisions, or baby care items. They were transported in cattle cars, packed like sardines, and those were the lucky ones—the rest were forced to travel on foot.

Lithuanian Jews were labeled as spies and traitors, and so Christian populations throughout their travels viewed them with suspicion, offering little to no aid.

An excerpt from "The Exile of the Lithuanian Jews during the Fervor of the First World War (1914–1918)," by Louis Stein.

In the Ponovezh old people's home, for example, there were 43 old

---

[3] See Appendix 1.

people. The youngest was an octogenarian and the oldest 99 years old. In Vilia a dying Jewish woman, Vilentschik, was laid in a wagon and ... later she died on the road. The husband of another dying woman, Pesye Fishelevitch, went to beg the police to allow him to stay with his wife until her last breath, but the police commissioner expelled him and his terminally ill wife was left alone in the shtetl to die.

The expulsions, splitting of families, starvation, and loss of family members produced numerous cases of mental derangement amongst the exiles, which then threatened to become epidemic.

Men had already been forcibly taken into the Russian army, at a rate considerably in excess of the ratio of Jews to the total population. So the majority of the deportees were women, children, and the elderly, "useless eaters," as the Nazi's would later define them—all defenseless against the prevailing authorities and local populations. A conservative estimate of the starving amongst the deportees was 600,000 people. Reports of rape, murder, and terrorization of these Jews is recorded. There were no authorities preventing these actions against these defenseless Jews by the local populations.

Jews were deported to indiscriminate locations, some recipient locations were so full of Jewish deportees that protests broke out upon the arrival of the exiles, and Jews were then forced on to different locations, thus increasing death rates. Food was scarce; Jewish aid societies sending food to the deportees was stopped by Railroad Detectives, who would search and steal the food in case "secret orders" were contained within. Government agents would travel to villages that were close to train stations and incite ignorant peasants against the exiled Jews. Hooligans were placed to wait for the trains containing "Jewish Traitors" so they could stone the starving, sick victims, thus ensuring even more suffering.

The Gochin family was part of the wandering hordes of starving and dispossessed Jews from 1915 to 1923.

GOCHIN FAMILY HISTORY

Sam Gochin was born in February 1902.His bar mitzvah would have been in February 1915; his deportation was 3 months later.

Whilst under deportation, at the tender age of 15, Sam was abducted and taken into the Russian army in Byelorussia in 1917.

The Russian Revolution of 1917 brought about legal equality for Jews in the Russian Empire. Many of the now itinerant Jews in Russia suffered through the civil war period of 1918–1920, many dying in the dreadful winter of 1919. White Guard gangs, operating against "Jewish Bolshevism" in heavily Lithuanian Jewish-populated southern Russia, murdered many Litvaks.[4]

Jews were expendable; it was common for competing warring European sides to put Jewish children in their frontlines, so that Jewish children were shooting at other Jewish children. All of this for a war that was never theirs, for wars in which they had no stake. During WWI, Nikolai Nikolaievitch and General Yanushkevitch ordered that all Army Commanders use Jewish soldiers as spearheads for every attack against the adversary, and during retreats, Jewish soldiers were to be in the last row,[5]thus ensuring maximum Jewish casualties. Government propaganda against Jews ensured that military compatriots gave Jews little, if any, military cover, thus subverting their own armies to ensure maximum Jewish death.

On February 16, 1918, Lithuania was declared an independent state, and slowly Jews began to attempt to return to their homes. Stories reached the exiles that Jews would be treated well in the new Lithuania. Jews worldwide supported Lithuanian independence to encourage the

---

[4] "The Exile of the Lithuanian Jews during the Fervor of the First World War (1914–1918)." Louis Stein.
[5] "The Exile of the Lithuanian Jews during the Fervor of the First World War (1914–1918)." Louis Stein.

future freedom and equality of Jews within Lithuania.

On July 12, 1920, the Soviet-Lithuanian Peace Treaty was signed between Lithuania and Soviet Russia. The Jewish National Council pressed for, and won, a clause in the peace accord stating that the Soviet government was obligated to transport, at their own expense, all those self-identified Lithuanian citizens who wished to return to Lithuania, and in August 1920, long trains loaded with returning Jews began the journey to repatriation. Returning was difficult, and not all were able to journey simultaneously. Sixty thousand Jews were in independent Lithuania, 100,000 Lithuanian Jews returned from the Soviet Union, resulting in a Lithuanian Jewish population of 160,000.

On December 26, 1921, Faive Gochin, father of Avram Gochin, submitted an application to the Lithuanian authorities to allow his son and family to return to Lithuania from their forced exile in Ukraine.

The Papile vital records had been destroyed on April 17, 1915, during the war, so Faive had to prove that his progeny were his progeny, and that they were Lithuanian.

Individual family testimonies were offered. The Papile Jewish community also supplied testimony that the Gochin family and children had been born in Papile.

CITIZENSHIP IN THE INDEPENDENT LITHUANIA

Citizenship legislation of the newly established state, in power since January 9, 1919, was generous. A constitution was drafted which defined citizenship as follows:

Citizens of Lithuania are the following registered persons:

- Those who live and lived in Lithuania, and whose parents and grandparents previously lived in Lithuania.

- Children of the persons mentioned above who did not currently live in Lithuania, but returned to live to Lithuania.

- Persons who lived in Lithuania not less than ten years before WWI and had property or permanent situation in Lithuania.

- Children of Lithuanian citizens.

- A wife or widow of a Lithuanian citizen.

- Illegitimate children of a Lithuanian citizen.

This was "generous" in that a male foreign spouse could become a Lithuanian citizen by virtue of marriage to a female Lithuanian citizen, or even, if that female Lithuanian citizen was now deceased, a foreign male could claim Lithuanian citizenship by virtue of marriage to a Lithuanian rights holder.

The law stated one set of legalities; Lithuanian bureaucrats implemented the law based on their own interpretations or their own ideologies.

APPLICATION TO RETURN TO LITHUANIA

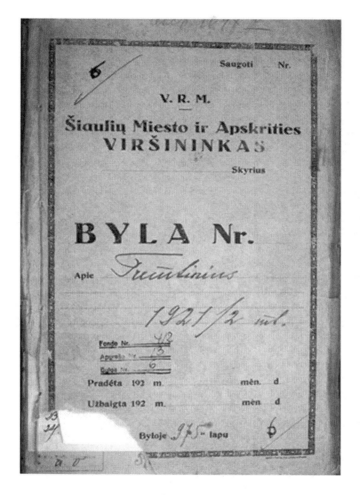

File Cover

Faive, father of Avram, applied for Chaie's return from Ukraine.

Avram, applied for Chaie's return.
Lithuanian State Central Archive _LCVA Fund 412, Inventory 13,
File 6 Page 857
Application By Faive Gochin, Dec.26, 1921.

Faive, father of Avram, applied for his children's return from Ukraine. He requested the return of the family of Avram Gochin from Russia, Province of Tavrichesky, town Melitopol (Ukraine).

Avram Gochin's family included his wife, Chaie; sons—Shmuel, Idel, and Yankel; and daughters—Esther and Leya.

Given their deportation in 1915, Faive did not know of all the family marriages and births. The list of children and grandchildren was not comprehensive.

Certificate from the Papile Jewish community issued in lieu of birth certificates on Dec. 20, 1921. Lithuanian State Central Archive _LCVA Fund 412, Inventory 13, File 6; Page 863

In order for them to be allowed to return, proof of citizenship was required. The Papile archives had been destroyed in WWI, so the re-formed Papile Jewish community issued a formal statement in lieu of birth certificates. This statement was issued on December 20, 1921 and was submitted with Faive's application.

It states:

The Gochin family is from Papile and lived there before WWI.

Avram (Sroel) Gochin was born in Papile on Nov. 13, 1866.

Chaie Gochin was born in Tryskiai (Trishik, in Yiddish) on Feb. 3, 1876.

Leya Gochin was born in Papile on Feb. 10, 1899.

Shmuel Gochin was born in Papile on Dec. 26, 1902.

Idel Gochin was born in Papile on Aug. 15, 1904.

Yankel Gochin was born in Papile on May 17, 1905.

Esther Gochin was born in Papile on May 18, 1909.

(It should be noted that the above are different dates of birth than were later reported by Sam, Jack, and Esther).

The dates of birth were offered from Faive's memory, as the people in question were not there—they were under deportation. In those days, people did not keep birth dates as they do today. They would have said things like, "He was born before Pesach in the year that xx was married." Therefore, dates of birth are seldom, if ever, consistent across

Jewish historical records.

Nineteenth-century vital records were recorded in the Russian Orthodox calendar, which differed from the Gregorian calendar of the twentieth century. (The Gregorian calendar added approximately 13 days in the twentieth century.)

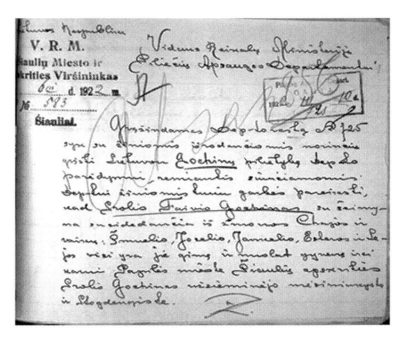

Lithuanian State Central Archive_LCVA Fund 412, Inventory 13, File 6; Page 856
From the Head of Shavl District to the Department of Citizens Security
By the Ministry of Interior,
March 6, 1922.

The council of Papile wrote to the head of the district confirming that there was no reason why the Gochin Family should not be allowed to return to Papile.

The council issued the following written statements:

They all were born in Papile and lived there until May 4, 1915 (the deportation date of Jews in Siauliai).

Avram Gochin's occupation was a butcher and roofer.

The Papile vital records were burned and destroyed during WWI, and there was no possibility of delivering those birth certificates.

Below is the certificate of the Papile Jewish community and the witness statements about the family of Avram Gochin of Papile.

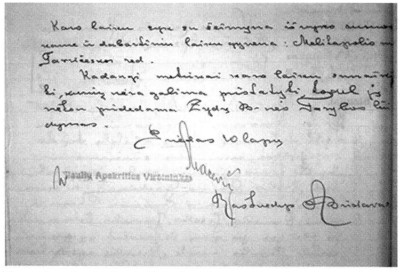

Lithuanian State Central Archive_LCVA Fund 412, Inventory 13, File 6; Page 856ap

The Council of Papile to the office of Head of Shavl District,

Feb. 28, 1922.

Lithuanian State Central Archive _LCVA Fund 412, Inventory 13, File 6;
Page 863

The council of Papile testified to the office of Head of Siauliai District, Feb 28, 1922.

They found no reasons why the Gochin family could not return to Lithuania.

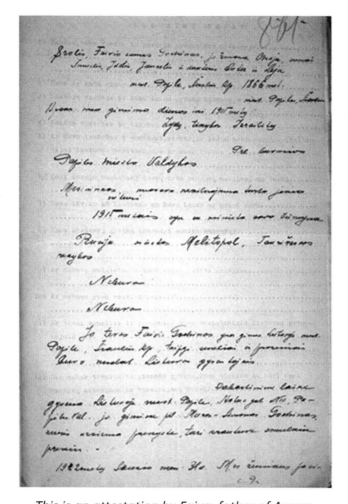

This is an attestation by Faiva, father of Avram.

Lithuanian State Central Archive _LCVA Fund 412, Inventory 13, File 6; Page 861

The attestation by Faive, father of Avram, reads:

Avram Gochin was born in Papile in 1866. He did not have any property.

His father, Faive Gochin, lived in Papile, on Stoties (Station) St. 10.

Their relative in Lithuania, Meyer Simon Gochin, lived in Papile. He is a tradesman and has a shop of small goods.

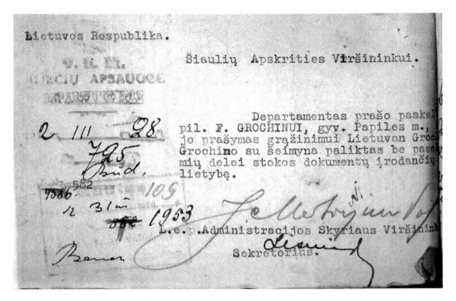

March 28, 1922

Lithuanian Department of Citizens Security.

Lithuanian State Central Archive _LCVA Fund 412, Inventory 13, File 6; Page 864

On March 28, 1922, the Lithuanian Department of Citizens Security, in a brief to the head of the Siauliai District, overturned the District findings and ruled that the Gochin family was not to be allowed to return to Lithuania. It stated that the Gochin Family lacked the documents to prove they were indeed Lithuanian.

In summary, the previous three documents illustrated clearly that Papile city council had testified that these were Lithuanian citizens, the official Jewish community had testified, and relatives had testified. Additionally, the Lithuanian Department of Citizens Security had been informed that the original documents were destroyed, this being a common occurrence. All this took place in independent Lithuania, a period during which Jews were promised equal rights as full Lithuanian citizens. It was supposed to be the Golden Age for Lithuanian Jews, since they had participated so heavily in the fight for independence, many of them giving their lives for the cause.

Jews fought alongside their fellow Lithuanian countrymen in the War of Independence, and provided full assistance wherever necessary.

Five hundred Jews were among 10,000 volunteers who answered the December 29, 1918, appeal of the Lithuanian government to defend the state from invaders.

Three thousand Jews served in the Lithuanian army from 1918 to 1923, and 23 of them were awarded the highest decoration—the Cross of Vytautas—for their outstanding service.

According to incomplete data, 73 Jews perished in battles. Jewish volunteers joined Lithuanians in the defense of Vilnius against the invading Polish forces.[6]

Jews began to return to Lithuania from their deportation after the war ended in 1919. The newly independent Lithuanian government set up repatriation centers to assist some Jews in returning; they wanted qualified Jews who could contribute to the new economy, but did they want all Jews? The answer is no.

---

[6]http://www.bernardinai.lt/straipsnis/2010-04-23-donatas-januta-lietuvos-karzygiai-lietuvos-zydai/43923

SOVIET ENFORCED STARVATIONS

Soviets had taken power in Russia after the 1917 revolution; Lenin and Stalin were on an expansionist quest in the region. One method they used was forced starvation in Ukraine in order to murder the peasants—yet another genocide attempt of the early twentieth century.

Between the fall of 1921 and the spring of 1923, an estimated 1.5–2 million people died of starvation and accompanying epidemics in Ukraine. The prime victims of famine and epidemics were children who were also the main targets for kidnappings and cannibalism. Given that the Baltic Jews were dispossessed and in deportation, they were not indigenous to the region and died in greater proportions. Word of the starvations and disease reached Lithuania and became widely known. Faiva submitted his application in Lithuania on December 26, 1921, for his family to be allowed to return. He was desperate; delay meant death.

Lithuanian government officials dithered and obfuscated the issues over how to refuse re-entry to some Jews. Jewish suffering and death was irrelevant to these officials, their objective was to rid themselves of superfluous Jews.

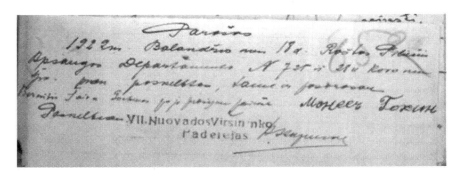

Notification

Lithuanian State Central Archive _LCVA Fund 412, Inventory 13, File 6;

Above is a notification that the outcome of Faive Gochin's application was announced to him. It reads: "For the illiterate Faive Gochin, receipt for this note was signed by Mones Gochin. Apr 18, 1922."

Mones (Faiva's son, Avram's brother) and his family had also been deported; he had returned from deportation on October 20, 1921.[7]

It took some time for Mones to return to Papile from the border crossing, and immediately upon his return, Mones and Faiva began work on the application for Avram's return, which was submitted with all documents two months and six days after Mones's return. Later, Mones and his family were murdered in the Holocaust.

Provable deaths in my family during deportation began with daughter Tsipa's husband, Jacob Skala,[8] on February 5, 1922, along with their daughter Deborah[9] on the same day.

Four days later, Chaie's husband, Avram,[10] died on February 9, 1922, along with their son Edel[11] on the same day.

Freyda Leya's husband, Gershon Ioselev Jankelev Ioffe,[12] and their two

---

[7] LCVA. F. 412. In. 13. File 12, The List of Deportees of the First World War. 1922–1923.

[8] Death Record: State Archive of Zaporizhska Oblast Record: P5593-17-11

[9] Birth Record: State Archive of Zaporizhska Oblast Record: P5593-1-233

[10] State Archive of Zaporozhye oblast: F. 5593. Inv. 17. File 11. "Gochil" (error), Israil Fayvelev, age 62, disabled, married, died in the 3d Soviet hospital 9/02/1922 (total exhaustion).

[11] Death Record: State Archive of Zaporizhska Oblast Record: P5593-17-11

[12] Marriage Record: State Archive of Zaporizhska Oblast, Ukraine: Date: 1 Sep 1918, Gochin Freyda-Leya Israileva, Ioffe Gershon Ioselev-Yankelev. Reference: Fund inventory dossier: P5593-1-243

children, Iosef[13] and Abram,[14] died on April 4, 1922. Their mother, Freyda Leya,[15] died one week later on April 11, 1922.

Tsipa[16] died on 6 June, 1922, four months and one day after her husband and daughter had died. Their son Max[17] survived; we will soon hear more about Max.

There are family legends of other grandchildren, but their names are lost to history.

Please think for a moment what it must have been like for Chaie, a girl from a small village, brutally deported, her husband, children, and grandchildren dying of starvation and disease around her, her son abducted, and still having living children to care for, whilst she herself must have been suffering from disease and starvation. Who among us would have the fortitude to continue, never mind the emotional capacity to survive? Could you endure what was done to Chaie?

Lithuanian authorities knew what was happening to the Lithuanian Jews in Ukraine, yet the Lithuanian government officials of the Ministry of the Interior refused re-entry based upon a "lack of documents." They knew that it was not possible to produce these documents, so the impossible documents became the only acceptable documents. This was a deliberate action on the part of the Lithuanian government. The question must be asked: "Is the Lithuanian government culpable in these deaths?"

---

[13] State Archive of Zaporizhska Oblast Record: 11.06.1919,,   Ioffe Gershon Ioselev, Gochin Freyda-Leya Israileva: P5593-1-233

[14] Death Record: State Archive of Zaporizhska Oblast Record: P5593-17-20

[15] Death records state buried in Melitopol, however the cemetery no longer exists.

[16] Marriage Record: State Archive of Zaporizhska Oblast, Ukraine: Date: 14 Jan 1919,   Skala Jakov Mordkovich, Gochin Tsipa Israileva, Reference: Fund inventory dossier: P5593-1-244

[17] Birth Record: State Archive of Zaporizhska Oblast Record: P5593-1-234

УКРАЇНА	UKRAINE
ЗАПОРІЗЬКА ОБЛАСНА	ZAPORIZHZHYA REGIONAL
ДЕРЖАВНА АДМІНІСТРАЦІЯ	STATE ADMINISTRATION
ДЕРЖАВНИЙ АРХІВ	STATE ARCHIVES
ЗАПОРІЗЬКОЇ ОБЛАСТІ	OF ZAPORIZHZHYA OBLAST

вул. Українська, 48, м. Запоріжжя, 69095
Тел. (0612) 621421, факс (0612) 622431
E-mail: dazo@zp.ukrtel.net
Web: http:// www.archivzp.gov.ua
Код ЄДРПОУ 03494617

Ukrainska Str., 48, Zaporizhzhya, 69095
Phone (0612) 621421, fax (0612) 622431
E-mail: dazo@zp.ukrtel.net
Web: http:// www.archivzp.gov.ua
USREOU Code 03494617

05.11.2012 № 01-34/7-337
На № _____ від _____

АРХІВНИЙ ВИТЯГ

ЗАЦС по м. Мелітополь
1922 р.

№ записи	Месяц и число смерти	Имя, отчество, фамилия род занятий умершего	Место смерти	Причи на смерти	Постоянное место жительства умершего	Возраст	Национальность	Семейное положение	Место погребения
395	16/II-1922	Гохиль Израиль Файвелев, нетрудо-способный	г. Мелитополь, 3 совет-ская больница	истоще ние	Ковенской губ. Шавель-ского у. м. Поволзн	62	еврей	женат	еврейское кладбище

Підстава: Р – 5593, оп. 17, спр 11, арк. 186 зв. – 187.

Директор   О.С. Тедеев

On February 9, 1922, Avram died of exhaustion / starvation in Melitopol, Ukraine. On that same day, his son Edel also died of starvation.

Above is the Ukrainian record of Avram's death, reflecting death from exhaustion or starvation.

CHAIE'S RETURN

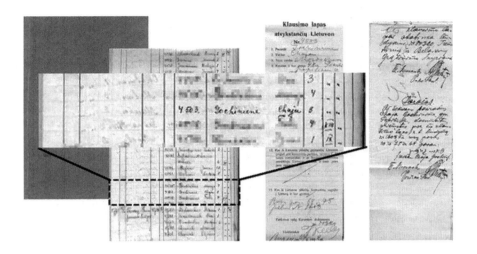

Chaie was determined to return to Lithuania after her seven-year forced exile.

Chaie's daughter Tsipa, her husband, Jacob, and daughter Deborah had all perished. At age 48, surrounded by death and despair, Chaie alone now had responsibility for her son Jack, daughter Esther, and grandson, Max, who was one-and-a-half years old.

Chaie began her trek back to Lithuania via the repatriation center in Kharkov. Along the way, Max fell ill and was hospitalized for two months. Chaie declined to leave him, as she knew that without her care, he too would die, so she kept the family waiting for two months, and then, on September 27, 1922, ignoring the denial of re-entry, she took her surviving children and grandchild to the Obeliai border crossing, completed her re-entry paperwork,[18] proved her Lithuanian citizenship, and was allowed to re-enter Lithuania.

---

[18] LCVA. F. 412. In. 13. File 12, The List of Deportees of the First World War. 1922–1923.

Above is Questionnaire Nr. 4503 of Sept. 27, 1922, answered by Chaie Gochiniene. This was the registration list of questionnaires of those heads of households returning from exile. Given that her husband, Avram, had died of starvation, Chaie was now the head of her household. This shows that Chaie Gochiniene (age 48), daughter of Mordekhay, was returning from Kharkov with her family. The family had five members—including toddler Max (fifth returnee unknown).

This questionnaire was sent by the head of Ezerenai Criminal Department to VIIth police precinct of Siauliai, which was responsible for Papile and its area. Ezerenai was the closest station to Obeliai. It was necessary to pass Ezerenai on the way from Russia to Lithuania. This procedure was used to check information which was given by returnees at the border. The questionnaire, with the other three documents, was sent to the police precinct for checking on Nov. 3, 1922.[19]

It was clear to the border guards in Obeliai that Chaie was a Lithuanian citizen and they allowed her in.

The Lithuanian government was suspicious of returnees, and so required inspection at the Obeliai crossing, where Jews were held in a concentrated area. Returning Jews were sometimes held for months at a time until they were released. Sanitary conditions were poor, and stories were told of mud, filth, and lice infestations, resulting in outbreaks of typhoid, and thus, more deaths.

Chaie returned to Papile to begin to rebuild her life. The pre-World War I Jewish community had numbered almost 1000 people; now it was decimated, given the massive death rates because of the deportations. When the Jews returned to Papile, they found their property destroyed and looted by their former neighbors, so they truly had to rebuild their lives. Stories were told of Lithuanian neighbors robbing Jewish homes

---

[19]LCVA. F. 412. In. 13. File. 12. L. 77 ap.) (LCVA. F. 412. In. 13. File. 13. L. 469.

before the Jews had finished being deported from Papile.

Many returning residents decided not to stay in Papile as there was now nothing there, and they moved to what they thought would be greener pastures. Of the 1000 pre-war Jewish residents, only about 200 Jews were in Papile in the late 1930s.

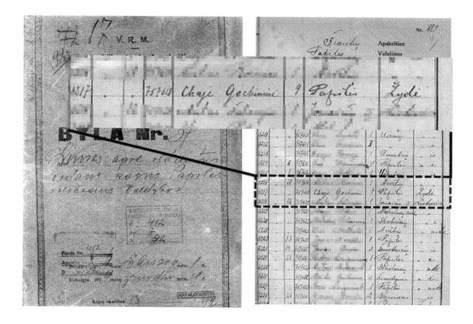

For the period 1919–1940, every Lithuanian citizen aged seventeen or older was required to have an internal passport.

Everybody was required to be registered; names were entered into registration books under the term "internal passports."

From the Lithuanian archives: On April 10, 1923, an internal passport of the Lithuanian Republic (Nr. 757619) was given to Chaje Gochiniene from Papile. Included in this passport were four minor children, (meaning the four children who had not yet reached 16–17 years of age at that time.[20] These children would have been Jack, Esther, Max, and one unknown). Note the line where Chaie's name appears—her nationality is stated as "Jewess." This line is highlighted.

Beginning in about 1922, any Jew that had not registered for an internal passport was to be deported from Lithuania. Recall that birth records

---

[20]File reference // LCVA. F. 412. In. 7. File. 75. P. 87; LCVA. F. 412. In. 7. File. 210. P. 4.

had deliberately been destroyed in order to prevent Jews from reclaiming their citizenship.

Here is a short article from the *Jewish Telegraphic Agency*, dated January 9, 1923:

"Expulsion of 'alien' Jews from Lithuania"[21]

Kowna (JTA)—The mass expulsion of "alien" Jews from Lithuania has recommenced. The official interpretation of alienage includes also Jews belonging to the Wilna district as well as the so-called occupied territory of Lithuania. Jews with records of long and continued residence and those who control large business are indiscriminately subjected to the expulsion act: the intervention of the Ministry for Jewish Affairs has proved futile.

---

[21]http://archive.jta.org/article/1923/01/09/2755061/expulsion-of-alien-jews-from-lithuania

In February 1926, Chaie's son Sam, at age 24, left for South Africa. Later the next month, on March 22, 1926, Faiva, father of Avram, died,[22] and now Chaie was even more alone.

Her son Jack left Lithuania to join Sam. Jack won a small amount of money in the Rhodesian lottery and sent it back to Lithuania for his mother, sister, and nephew. Chaie obtained an external passport and listed her grandson, Max, as her son. This was easy for her to do since no records existed as to who belonged to whom, and few facts were provable. There was no formal adoption process.

Chaie, Esther, and Max left Lithuania together and traveled to South Africa, arriving in April 1930. After all her suffering, she wasn't able to get to South Africa in time to enjoy Sam's wedding, which took place in 1929.

Had Jack not won the lottery, we shall shortly see what would have become of Chaie, Esther, and Max, because for the Jews that did not leave, there was far, far worse to come.

---

[22] LCVA F. 412. In. 5. File 1302. P. 595 ap and 596

SAM'S STORY

Now we shift to the story of Samuel Gochin of Papile. According to him, he was born on February 15, 1902. His South African identity number was 020215-5010-004, the first six numbers reflecting his date of birth: 020215—1902 February 15.

Sam was thirteen when he was first deported.

In 1917, at age fifteen, Sam was abducted and taken into the Russian army in Byelorussia to fight their war. Initially he was taken by the

Whites, then by the Reds, and then by the Whites again.

In 1918, Belarus was occupied first by the Germans, and then by the Poles. Whoever was the ruling authority at that moment had military control over conscripts.

During all these abductions, by one military after another, Sam was never asked his date of birth. If he was a living body that was able to absorb one of their enemy bullets, he was a worthwhile target for military abduction.

WWI ended in 1919, and Sam probably made his way back to Lithuania around 1922–23.

Samuel Gochin
5th Grand Duke Kestutis Doughboys Troop
Lithuania
1924

In 1924, the army of independent Lithuania was operational. It had started to operate after the Independent Republic of Lithuania was created.

Published rules stated that men of age twenty were to be mobilized for military service. In the first years, the system did not work perfectly—men who were conscripted were approximately that age.

Just as Sam had been a target for the other armies, so too was he a target for the Lithuanian army, and for the fourth time in his young life, he was taken by a military regime that cared naught for his wellbeing.

Lithuania was divided into the regions where separate Divisions of the army were physically located. Men were generally sent to troop nearest to their place of residence. Sam was from Papile—in the second quarter of 1924, Sam, having survived three militaries, was conscripted into the Lithuanian army by the Recruitment Commission of Siauliai District.

The number on Sam's military uniform shoulder was 5. This means his military place of service was Kaunas, the 5th Grand Duke Kestutis Doughboys Infantry Troop.

The location of the Lithuanian army troop building was in Aukstoji Panemune, a sub district of Kaunas; it had previously been a Tsarist army building.

Professor Dr. Jonis Vaicenonis, vice-dean of humanities at Vytautas Magnus University and chairman of Lithuania's War History Association, independently determined the data regarding Sam's Lithuanian military experience. He was provided with photographs of Sam, and from the epaulettes in the photographs, the professor identified Sam's military unit, and from there found Sam's military file in the Lithuanian archives.

Having endured starvation and illness, Sam was still physically weak,
and on June 6, 1924, Sam was registered as a patient at the War
Hospital of Jonas Basanavicius, in Kaunas. In his case record from the
hospital, Lithuanian military doctors recommended that he be released
from service due to his physical condition. Military medical
recommendations were not binding on military leaders, and so the
military leadership declined the recommendations, forcing him to serve

the entire eighteen months they required. After all, why would Lithuania consider the needs of a Jew?

Sam was freed from service at the end of 1925.

LCVA. F.1102. In 2. File55. P. 101 ap

Above are Sam's medical records.

The records read: "The patient was of medium height and medium constitution. He had an ache on the left side of the top of his breast. He was spitting blood. His bronchial breathing was too long and phlegmy."

X-rays showed that there were unclear spots on the top of his left lung, but tuberculosis was not found.

The doctors recommended that Sam be placed in the Recruit Reserves.

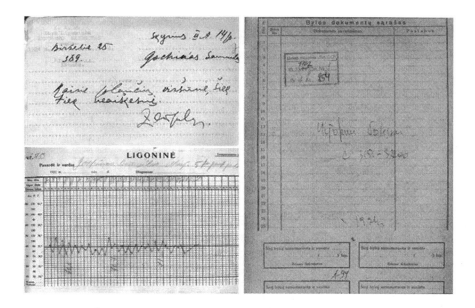

Here we see additional records from Sam's Lithuanian military medical files. Note his daily temperature readings.

Sam told his grandchildren how he learned to play a musical instrument whilst in the military hospital. Here are two photographs of him in the military hospital; the back one shows him in a musical group.

The military was segregated. Jews did not speak much Lithuanian; they spoke primarily Yiddish, and of course the ethnic Lithuanians spoke no Yiddish.

SAM'S POST MILITARY LIFE

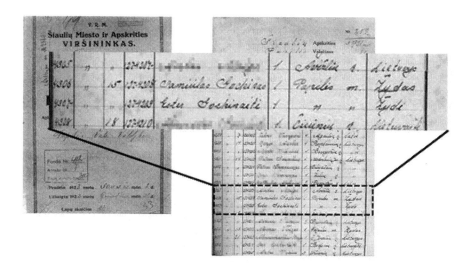

Sam was required to apply for an internal passport—the term used for an identity document. He went with his younger sister, Esther, to apply.

Above are the records—first Sam listed as Jew, and immediately underneath him, Esther listed as Jewess. Compare the line above Sam's, where that person's nationality is listed as Lithuanian.

On November 5, 1924, in Papile, Sam was issued his internal passport of the Lithuanian Republic.[23]

---

[23](Nr. 767121) - file // LCVA. F. 412. In. 7. File. 92. P. 16

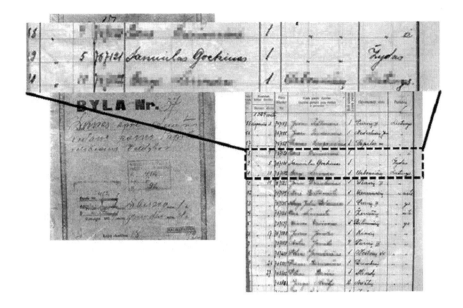

On Jan 15, 1926, another internal passport of the Lithuanian Republic (Nr. Nr.127 - 4208)was issued to Samuel Gochin from Papile// LCVA. F. 412. In. 8. File. 325. p. 16

Sam was issued another internal passport on January 15, 1926. By that time Sam had already completed his military service, so perhaps he had lost his first internal passport during his military service.

It was not difficult to obtain a replacement passport since he had already been recognized as a citizen of Lithuania. This second internal passport was issued before he left Lithuania.

Much of Sam's correspondence from those years remains. By 1923, Sam was receiving cards from relatives, where the tone indicates that people were saying good-bye. There could have been many reasons why Sam did not emigrate earlier. Perhaps one of the reasons could be military service. People wishing to leave Lithuania had to collect numerous documents from the municipality and courts. But first they had to obtain a foreign passport. To obtain a passport, people had to give the authorities documents that could confirm their age, descent, residence, and occupation. If men could not obtain a birth certificate from their birthplace, military recruitment commission documents were accepted.

According to the rules, Sam had to return his internal passport before leaving the country.

No. 12475.

INDEXED.

UNION OF SOUTH AFRICA.

British Nationality in the Union and Naturalization and Status of Aliens Act, 1926.

CERTIFICATE OF NATURALIZATION.

Whereas SAMUEL GOCHIN

of Port Elizabeth

in the Province of the Cape of Good Hope, Union of South Africa,

has applied for a Certificate of Naturalization, alleging with respect to himself the particulars set out below, and has satisfied the Minister that the conditions laid down in the above-mentioned Act for the grant of a Certificate of Naturalization are fulfilled in his case, and intends, when naturalized to continue to reside within the Union of South Africa:

And whereas the said SAMUEL GOCHIN has made and subscribed the Oath of Allegiance to His Majesty the King, His Heirs and Successors:

Now, therefore, in pursuance of the powers conferred on him by the said Act, the Minister grants to the said SAMUEL GOCHIN

this Certificate of Naturalization, and declares that the said SAMUEL GOCHIN shall, subject to the provisions of the Act, be henceforth entitled to all political and other rights, powers, and privileges, and be subject to all obligations, duties, and liabilities to which a natural-born British subject is entitled or subject, and have to all intents and purposes the status of a natural-born British subject.

By order of the Minister.

P. I. HOOGENHOUT.
Secretary for the Interior.

2 July 19 31.

Signature of holder

Signed in my presence

(Insert Official Designation.)

Place

Date

Particulars Relating to Holder.

Full name	SAMUEL GOCHIN
Address	41 Green Street, Port Elizabeth.
Trade or occupation	General Dealer.
Place and date of birth	Papile, Siauliai, Lithuania, : 15th February, 1902.
Nationality	Lithuanian
Married, single, or widower (widow)	Married
Name of wife	Dora Bommel.
Names of parents	Abraham Ismael Gochin and Chaie Turk.
Nationality of parents	Lithuanian

Sam's Certificate of Naturalization.

Sam left Lithuania in February 1926, traveling via London, and connected to the ship *Gaika* on February 25, 1926. He was twenty-four years old, and had survived deportations, starvation, and four different militaries. He reached Cape Town on March 21, 1926, and arrived into

Port Elizabeth on March 25, 1926. He had traveled for a month in third class.

Sam's mother, Chaie, and sister Esther left Lithuania for South Africa in 1930, taking along Chaie's grandson, Max, who would henceforth be identified as her own son.

Sam later told his grandchildren that South Africa was the "Golden Medina"—the land where Jews could live in peace.

Sam was naturalized as a South African citizen on July 28, 1931. He proudly stated his nationality as Lithuanian and showed his parents' nationality as Lithuanian.

WHAT HAPPENED TO THE REMAINING JEWS OF PAPILE?

What happened to the Jews that never managed to leave Papile?[24]

"Mass Murder of Jews from the Siauliai region in Zagare"

---

[24]http://www.holocaustatlas.lt/EN/#a_atlas/search/bendri=Papile.vietove=.aukos=.from_year=0.from_month=0.from_day=.to_year=0.to_month=0.to_day=.killers=/page/1/item/106/

About Massacre

"In late July 1941, the activists made a list of Jews who stayed in Zagare and began to transfer them to the ghetto. The Jews who lived in nearby *shtetls* were also moved to the ghetto of Zagare. The area chosen for the ghetto adjoined the market place and included Daukanto, Vilniaus, Maluno, Pakalnio, and Gedimino streets. Non-Jewish residents of these streets were moved to other neighborhoods. On August 22, chief of the Siauliai region **Jonas Noreika** informed local authorities and mayors of smaller towns of the Siauliai region that according to the order of the Siauliai *Gebietskommissar*, all the region's Jews and half-Jews were obliged to move to Zagare by August 29. The transfer began with Jews from Siauliai, Joniskis, Kursenai, Zeimelis, and other localities. On August 25, the mayor of Zagare informed the regional chief of Siauliai that the ghetto occupied an area of 12,135 square meters and had a population of 715 Jews.

"By August 29, 949 Jews from other localities in the Siauliai region had been moved to Zagare: from Tryskiai, women and children; Siaulenai, 60–70 families; Saukenai, women and children; Radviliskis, women and children; Pasvintinys, 70 people; Papile, women and children; Kursenai, a few hundred (about 50 carriages with women, children, and old people); Gruzdziai, women, children, and old people; and from Joniskis, 150 people. On September 20, 5,566 people (2,402 Jews and 3,164 non-Jews) resided in Zagare.

"In the last days of September 1941, several local ethnic Lithuanians were marched to the town park (formerly Count Naryshkin's Park) where they were forced to dig a ditch in the shape of an L (120 meters long, two to three meters wide and two meters deep). On the morning of October 2, Jews from the Zagare ghetto were ordered to gather in the market square. Commandant Mannteuffel addressed the crowd in German, assuring them that they would all be given work to do. The Jewish men, women, children, and elderly people had to form separate lines. When the German whistle blew, white armbanders and policemen from Zagare and other towns began to surround the square. Panic arose among the Jews and some tried to escape. The armbanders shot into the crowd and beat them. Scores of killed and wounded people were left on the square. The survivors were forced to lie down on the ground where they had to stay until several trucks arrived. Jews were then transported to Naryshkin Park.

"Money, jewelry, and other valuables were seized from the Jews as they marched to the murder site. At the ditch, the victims had to remove everything except their underwear before they were forced to lie down in the pit and were shot. The executioners were a self-defense unit from Siauliai, led by Lieutenant R. Koloska and white armbanders from Linkuva. The Zagare white armbanders guarded the ghetto and led the victims to their deaths. Several German SS men who had arrived from Siauliai supervised the killings and also participated in them.

"The mass murder continued until very late at night. On the following day another group of Jews who had been discovered and seized were brought to the park and murdered in the same ditch.

"The report issued by German Security Police Chief and the SD in Lithuania SS-*Standartenfuhrer* Karl Jager stated that on October 2, 1941, 2,236 Jews (663 men, 1,107 women, and 496 children) were killed in Zagare. During the panic which arose at the market square before the executions, 150 Jews were killed and seven white armbanders who guarded them were wounded. The Soviet special commission, who examined the mass grave in 1944, found 2,402 corpses (530 men, 1,223 women, 625 children, and 24 infants)."

Address: **Zagare town, Kestuciog. street, Joniskis district**

Victim number: **2236-24**

Perpetrators

Commandant of the Zagare ghetto Mannteuffel;

German SS men;
Zagare white armbanders and policemen;
Siauliai unit of the Siauliai battalion;
Linkuva white armbanders

Honors given to Noreika[25]

In 2010, the primary school in Sukoniai in the Pakruojis region was named for him.

Library of the Academy of Sciences in Vilnius has a plaque installed for him in the front of the building.

A symbolic grave and a statue of him were set up in Antakalnis Cemetery in Vilnius right next to the memorial to the victims of January 13, 1991.

In Kaunas, there is a street named for him: Generolo Vetros gatve.

---

[25]http://atminimas.kvb.lt/asmenvardis.php?asm=GENEROLAS%20V%C
BTRA,%20tikrasis%20vardas%20%96%20kpt.%20Jonas%20Noreika

WORLD WAR II IN LITHUANIA

From right to left: Adolf Hitler, Lithuanian Ambassador Colonel Skirpa, and Lithuanian military attaché to Germany, General Rastikis.

On page 26, we addressed citizenship in independent Lithuania; we now transition to examining citizenship during the Second World War.

Russians invaded in 1940 and left in 1941. For about six weeks, Lithuania was ruled by the interim Lithuanian Provisional Government under the auspices of the German government.

The founder of the Lithuanian Activist Front (LAF) was Colonel Skirpa, and the interim prime minister of the provisional government was Brazaitis.

An excerpt from the platform of the LAF and the provisional government of Lithuania, June 23, 1941–August 5, 1941, reads:

Lithuanian brothers and sisters!

The final hour of reckoning with the Jews has arrived. Lithuania must be liberated not only from the enslavement of the Asiatic Bolsheviks, but also from the prolonged yoke of Jewry. In the name of the entire Lithuanian nation, the Lithuanian Activist Front most ceremoniously declares:

1. The ancient right of sanctuary extended to the Jews by Vytautas the Great is canceled completely and finally.

2. Every Jew of Lithuania without exception is officially warned to quit the land of Lithuania immediately and without any delay.

3. Jews are eliminated from Lithuania completely and forever.

And with this, approximately 96.4 percent of Jews on the territory of Lithuania were murdered, the highest murder rate of any country in Europe. It was safer to be a Jew in Nazi Germany than it was to be a Jew in Lithuania. By the beginning of 1942, 80 percent of the Jewish population of Lithuania had already been murdered, oftentimes without any German presence. There was vigorous and widespread participation of the Lithuanian population in the murder of Jews and the plunder of their possessions, the plundering taking place even before the butchering had finished. Einsatzkommando 2 of the German security police reported the murder of 114,856 Lithuanian Jews as early as December 1, 1942. This was accomplished with only 139 personnel, of whom 44 were secretaries and drivers.[26] Ninety-five murderers had sufficient assistance from local Lithuanians to murder 114,856 Jews in just a few months.

In minute No. 5, from June 27,1941 of the LAF, it is recorded that "Minister Zemkalnis reported on the unusually brutal massacres committed against Jews in Kaunas, at the Lietukis garage:

---

[26] Timothy Snyder, *Bloodlands*. (Basic Books, 2010), 192.

It is resolved that, despite all the measures to be taken against the Jews for their Communist activities and harm caused to the German army, the partisans and individual citizens should avoid public executions of Jews."

No. 6 of the June 30, 1941 (on the establishment of the Lithuanian police battalion) minutes reads, in part:

2. To approve the establishment of the Jewish concentration camp, instructing its guidance and creation to Vice-Minister of Communal Utilities Mr. Svilpa in cooperation with Mr. Colonel Bobelis.

The concentration camp was established at Kaunas's Seventh Fort. Using the provisional government's money, the Lithuanian battalion there started the regulated destruction of Jews. Until the concentration camp closed on September 10, 1941, Lithuanian battalion servicemen murdered about five thousand Jews of Kaunas.

On August 1, 1941—four days prior to the termination of its activities— the provisional government received approval for Lithuania's "Regulation on Jews." It is the Lithuanian version of the "final solution of the Jewish question."

The LAF announced from the Kaunas radio center about the establishment of the provisional government, which said:

Brothers Lithuanians! Take your weapons and help the German army in the cause of national liberation. With confidence and grateful joy meet the marching German troops and provide them with all possible assistance. Long live the friendly relations with the great Germany and its leader Adolf Hitler! Long live free and independent Lithuania!

The interim prime minister of Lithuania, Brazaitis, who signed the orders to create the first Jewish ghettos, and who suggested that Jews not be murdered "so publicly," was re-buried in Lithuania in May 2012 with full state honors. This re-burial was funded by the office of the Lithuanian prime minister.

The Lithuanian Activist Front stoked the murderous flames and was a willing and zealous partner of the Nazis. During the LAF's 43 days of existence, the provisional government issued numerous anti-Semitic laws that began the initial stages of the "final solution" of Lithuanian Jewry.

In 1995, Skirpa was re-buried in Lithuania. The memorial speeches were given by the then prime minister of Lithuania, Adolfas Slezevicius, and Defense Minister Linas Linkevicius (who became minister of foreign affairs in 2012). The Lithuanian national anthem, as well as the military salute, followed.

After WWII, Germany and Austria "de-Nazi-fied." After re-independence, Lithuania turned her Jew murderers into national heroes.

On September 12, 2000, the Lithuanian Seimas voted for the legitimacy of the 1941 provisional government of Lithuania.

Not a single Lithuanian Holocaust perpetrator has been punished in Lithuania since it became independent.

The founder of the LAF, Colonel Kazys Skirpa, has been honored with streets named for him—K. Skirpa Street (gatve), in Kaunas. There is also a K. Skirpos aleja (alley), in Vilnius.

Imagine if the city of Berlin named one of its main streets Adolph Hitler Street, or if the street in front of the Twin Towers in New York were renamed Osama Bin Laden Street. Imagine the revulsion this would elicit from any civilized human being? Yet twenty-first century Lithuania has no issues with honoring murderers.

I know of no streets named for anybody that rescued Jews in Lithuania, only of streets named for those that were culpable of Jewish murder. For some unknown reason, when the Lithuanian Ministry of Foreign Affairs announces how they mourn their murdered Jews, and they seek Jewish investment and tourism, they somehow neglect to mention such recent honors as naming a school for Noreika, or the state re-burial of Brazaitis. I wonder why that is?

The honoring of Brazaitis, Noreika, and Skirpa in Lithuania are NOT isolated incidents.[27]

Following area few other examples of Lithuania's sincerity in their statements that they mourn the murder of their Jews. Civilized people cannot name streets in Lithuania; civilized people may only interpret current Lithuanian moral values by those that Lithuania holds up as examples.

1. Brazaitis—lecture hall at Vytautas Magnus University, Kaunas.

---

[27]Photos from http://defendinghistory.com/memorials-to-holocaust-collaborators-in-public-spaces-and-state-sponsored-institutions-in-lithuania

2: Brazaitis—bas-relief at Vytautas Magnus University, Kaunas.

3. Baltusis-Zvejas Street, Kaunas—during the war, Baltusis-Zvejas was in command of Lithuanian police who guarded the Maidanek concentration camp where more than 79,000 people were killed or starved to death.

4. Juozas Krikstaponis square in Ukmerge—this Lithuanian hero was in command of a unit responsible for murdering tens of thousands of Jews in Belarus.

5. Noreika—(previously addressed). This inscription is high on the facade of the Genocide Museum, located on the main boulevard of Vilnius; the museum barely mentions the genocide of the Jews of Lithuania.

6. Noreika—street name in Kaunas.

7. Noreika—on the Siauliai Region government building.

8. Skirpa—street name in Kaunas.

And so continues the dichotomy of the Lithuanian Ministry of Foreign Affairs shedding false tears for murdered Jews, while simultaneously requesting Jewish investment in Lithuania and Jewish tourism to Lithuania, and according monuments and honors to the murderers.

Note that these dictates are the actions of the Lithuanian government. Nobody should stereotype the Lithuanian people. The Lithuanian education system has gaps, and the general population is mostly unaware of the actions of those who are awarded false honors

LITHUANIAN RE-INDEPENDENCE

Lithuania regained independence from the Soviet Union on March 11, 1990.

The newly independent state offered citizenship to those descendants of Lithuanian citizens who had not repatriated. If a Jew had gone to Israel, it was considered that the Jew had repatriated to his or her home country and therefore lost the right to citizenship in Lithuania, i.e. the law distinguished rights based upon ethnicity. Recall that in the internal passport records, Jews were not Lithuanian, just Jews.

Lithuania instituted a law of restitution, which stated in paragraph 2, section 1, that private property could be claimed only by Lithuanian citizens.

Chapter 3 of the same paragraph reads: "If one has lost his citizenship only between 1939 to 1990, then only his spouse and children (nobody further) are eligible to claim property."

Private Property
The Lithuanian claims process for restitution of property seized under the laws of the USSR or otherwise unlawfully nationalized, established under the Restoration of the Rights of Ownership of Citizens to Existing Real Property law (enacted in 1997 and amended in 2002), provided that former property owners, and certain heirs, were eligible to recover their confiscated property, so long as claimants were Lithuanian resident citizens.

But what if they were now American citizens?[28-29]

The key term in the constitutional provision of Article 23 is "rights of

---

[28]http://www.wjro.org.il/Web/Operations/Lithuania/Default.aspx

[29]http://www3.lrs.lt/pls/inter3/dokpaieska.showdoc_l?p_id=412725

ownership."

In 1994, Lithuania enacted the Law on Land, establishing a basic definition of the term *ownership* as providing the "authority to manage the owned land and dispose of it without violating the laws of the Republic or the rights or legitimate interests of other persons."

The "right to ownership," however, was an entirely different concept than ownership.

On May 27, 1994, Lithuania's Constitutional Court clarified that property nationalized by the Soviet authorities since 1940 was "under *de facto* control of the state."

Consequently, although former owners were entitled to ownership of land under the Law on Land, they lacked the rights of ownership until such time that a competent authority made a final decision to restitute the property or to provide compensation.

In other words, former owners do not possess any ownership rights in their wrongfully expropriated land until the Lithuanian government formally grants such rights.

The law of restitution provided for the restitution of land and buildings, which had been confiscated by the Soviet regime between 1940 and 1950, to *citizens* and their descendants.[30]

See pages 10, 11, 12, 17:
http://www.kentlaw.edu/jicl/articles/spring2011/Stovall_Note.pdf

Former citizens and their heirs were deprived of their property, not because of the new constitution, but as a consequence of Parliament's adoption—and the court's application—of the law of restitution that limited claims to citizens only.

---

[30]http://www.kentlaw.edu/jicl/articles/spring2011/Stovall_Note.pdf

Legislation on private property stated that restitution applications had to be submitted by 2001, and only by resident citizens, but that dual citizenship was not allowed. So to claim restitution of one's stolen property, one would have had to renounce American citizenship, relocate to Lithuania, and become a Lithuanian citizen.

Momentarily we will see how the Lithuanian Interior Ministry responded to citizenship applications by Jews. In marketing to descendants of Lithuanian Jews, they proudly state that they made restitution; it's just the devil in the details that goes missing.

Lithuania faced great pressure by her expatriate population to allow for dual citizenship—in order for expatriates to maintain ties to their country of heritage. This presented a challenge to Lithuania in that, if it were allowed, would Litvaks want property returned?

Later there was a small re-opening of the restitution window, however, it proved to be extraordinarily complex. In general, a municipality held possession of private property, so when one filed for property, it was rejected, and the applicant customarily lost in court. Claimants would then appeal to a higher court, and win, however, the municipality also appealed to the higher court, and so complicating the situation. Therefore, very few people were granted restitution by a higher court. One would assume that a court in a democratic, civilized, European country would rule based upon objective facts, and the rule of law, however, this was not usually the case.

We have already seen from Chaie's situation in 1922 how deceptive the Lithuanian government can be. We will now see an example of the treatment of Jews under the new modern, independent, and democratic State of Lithuania.[31]

---

[31]http://www3.lrs.lt/home/Konstitucija/Constitution.htm

In the 1915 deportations, Jewish property was stolen by the Russians. In 1940, Jewish property was stolen by the Soviets. In 1941, Jewish property was stolen by the Nazis, and now we see the newly independent state of Lithuania making every effort NOT to restitute Jewish property.

Is holding stolen property considered a crime in 2013?

Given expatriate pressure for dual citizenship, Lithuania issued an amendment to their citizenship law on December 2, 2010. This amendment allowed dual citizenship for those who had been forcibly exiled after June 15, 1940.

But yet again, the devil is in the details. Those who left voluntarily prior to that date were not entitled to dual citizenship, and therefore not entitled to claim restitution. This included all the Jews, because if you were a Jew in Lithuania after June 15, 1940, you ended up here—in Ponary, the killing fields just outside Vilnius. Given a 96.4 percent murder rate of Lithuanian Jews, the likelihood of a Jew surviving only to be "forcibly exiled" after June 15, 1940, was close to nil.

Lithuania had succeeded in creating a dual citizenship law that excluded Jews, without having to define it as such, and therefore, exempting them from claiming the return of stolen property.

A common government ploy, particularly in cases of anti-Semitism, is delay, deny, and obfuscate. An example relating to the U.S.:

Why did millions die in the Holocaust? Here's one reason: In 1940, the United States' immigration policy was governed by Under Secretary of State Breckinridge Long, who declared, "We can delay and effectively stop for a temporary period of indefinite length the number of immigrants into the United States. We could do this by simply advising our consuls to put every obstacle in the way and to require additional evidence and to resort to various administrative devices which would postpone and postpone and postpone the granting of the visas."

In the case of Chaie Gochin, we witnessed the delays, obfuscations, and deceit by the independent state of Lithuania. Surely, in the twenty-first century, that would be a thing of the past, especially by a member state of the European Union?

GRANT'S STORY

Now we turn to my journey with the government of Lithuania.

The Jewish cemetery in Papile had been destroyed. Where hundreds of Gochins had likely been buried, only four stones remained. Above is a photograph of my son, Bryce Gochin-Lyon, saying Kaddish at the new gravestone I installed in Papile to memorialize all the Gochins who had come from that village.

In this photograph, my then eleven-year-old son holds a copy of the book I created as a bar mitzvah gift for him, to document and memorialize my relatives. My grandfather Sam was only two years older than my son is in this photo when he was deported. Bryce's Hebrew name is Shmuel, to honor my grandfather; Bryce was born on February 15, 2001, exactly to the date 99 years after Sam's date of birth.

Sam's youngest son was Harold. Below we see Harold's South African birth certificate showing his father, Samuel Gochin, age thirty-one, born in Lithuania.

In the 1930s, people were not overly date conscious, so Sam may well have been born any time between June 14, 1901 and June 12, 1903, for him to be thirty-one years of age when Harold was born. We know that Sam noted his date of birth as February 15, 1902.

When the Papile Jewish community had written their statement, in which somebody had to make up a date of birth for Sam, they used December 26, 1902.

Below is my birth certificate, showing me as the son of Harold. I was born in 1963; even then there was not a firm consciousness of dates. Instead of birth dates for parents, rounded ages were given.

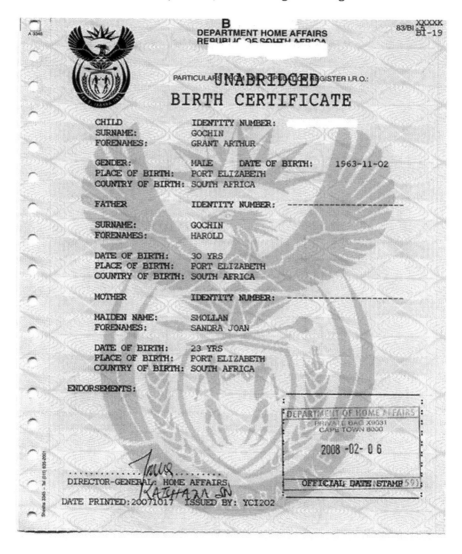

A direct line—Sam was born in Lithuania; his son Harold was born in South Africa; his grandson Grant (me) was born in South Africa. There is nothing confusing or ambiguous in these documents.

In 2004, when dual Lithuanian citizenship was available, I applied. My grandfather had strongly identified as a Litvak—he always spoke of his Lithuanian heritage—and I wanted a tangible sign of Lithuania to pass onto my son, so that generations from now, when my son's descendants asked how they came to hold Lithuanian citizenship, the name Sam Gochin would be spoken, and his memory would be kept alive. A very sentimental reason, but I had no idea where this journey would lead me.

Recall that Faiva was illiterate. In his tax records I have found that he was listed as "poor." Avram had died from starvation, and Sam left young. There was no property for me to claim, no ulterior reason for claiming citizenship—this was a purely emotional quest.

THE APPLICATION

On the next page is a copy of my application. Note question #4—I was REQUIRED to state my nationality. That is no longer a term in common usage, so I asked the Lithuanian official what exactly they meant: should I enter South African, or American, or even Lithuanian, as my grandfather had on his South African naturalization certificate?

The Lithuanian official's answer shocked me. He said I was required to state my nationality as "Jew." I questioned this, and he explained that a Jew was a Jew, a Lithuanian was a Lithuanian, and that they were different; a Jew could not be Lithuanian and vice versa, so my nationality was clearly "Jew."

I declined to answer "Jew," so again he explained that it was required, and that if I did not write "Jew," my application would be considered fraudulent. Very reluctantly, I filed as a Jew.

Citizenship application for Grant Gochin, dated December 2004.

In line #3, above, it shows my place of birth as Pietu Afrika (South Africa). The Lithuanian Ministry of Foreign Affairs openly acknowledges that about 90 percent of South African Jews are of Lithuanian origin, therefore, when the Lithuanian Migration Department (a division of the Ministry of the Interior) receives a citizenship application from a South

African Jew, there should naturally be an assumption that 90 percent of the case has already been concluded. Apparently the outwardly facing Ministry of Foreign Affairs and the individual-facing Ministry of the Interior do not share the same data, so let us put aside all assumptions and look at the adjudication of the documents.

As we review this together, I ask you to recall what the Lithuanian government did with my great-grandmother in 1922, when they denied her citizenship and her right to re-entry.

GRANT ARTHUR GOCHIN

CITIZENSHIP DENIAL

MIGRACIJOS DEPARTAMENTO
PRIE LIETUVOS RESPUBLIKOS VIDAUS REIKALŲ MINISTERIJOS
PILIETYBĖS REIKALŲ SKYRIUS

SPRENDIMAS
DĖL GRANT ARTHUR GOCHIN LIETUVOS RESPUBLIKOS PILIETYBĖS

2007 m. birželio 18 d. Nr. (15/3-11) 8P-615
Vilnius

Migracijos departamento prie Vidaus reikalų ministerijos Pilietybės reikalų skyrius išnagrinėjo Grant Arthur Gochin prašymą ir dokumentus dėl Lietuvos Respublikos pilietybės.
Grant Arthur Gochin gimė 1963-11-02 Pietų Afrikos Respublikoje, Port Elisabeth. Asmuo gyvena Jungtinėse Amerikos Valstijose. G. A. Gochin yra Jungtinių Amerikos Valstijų ir Pietų Afrikos pilietis – atitinkamai tai patvirtina Jungtinių Amerikos Valstijų piliečio pasas Nr. 038735574, išduotas 2004-02-10 Los Andželo pasų agentūros, ir Pietų Afrikos Respublikos piliečio pasas Nr. 403263718, išduotas 1997-02-11 Vidaus reikalų ministerijos.
G. A. Gochin pateikė dokumentus senelio Samuilo (Samuelio) Gochino iki 1940-06-15 turėtai Lietuvos pilietybei įrodyti.
Vadovaudamasi Lietuvos Respublikos pilietybės įstatymo 1 straipsnio 1 punktu, 26 straipsnio 4 dalimi, 28 straipsnio 7 dalimi, 32 straipsnio 1 dalimi, vidaus reikalų ministro 2006-04-24 įsakymu Nr. IV-154 „Dėl Lietuvos Respublikos vidaus reikalų ministro 2003 m. sausio 23 d. įsakymo Nr. 1V-29 „Dėl įgaliojimų suteikimo" pakeitimo". 2006-05-03 Migracijos departamento prie Vidaus reikalų ministerijos direktoriaus įsakymu Nr. 3K-47 „Dėl įgaliojimų suteikimo", atsižvelgdama į 2006-11-13 Lietuvos Respublikos Konstitucinio Teismo nutarimą „Dėl teisės aktų, reguliuojančių Lietuvos Respublikos pilietybės santykius, nuostatų atitikties Lietuvos Respublikos Konstitucijai". 2007-06-15 Migracijos departamento prie Vidaus reikalų ministerijos Pilietybės reikalų skyriaus vyresniosios specialistės išvadą „Dėl Grant Arthur Gochin Lietuvos Respublikos pilietybės" Nr. (15/3-11) 3P-443 bei pateiktus dokumentus,

n u s p r e n d ž i u:

1. Pripažinti, kad Grant Arthur Gochin, gim. 1963-11-02 Pietų Afrikos Respublikoje, Port Elisabeth., nėra Lietuvos Respublikos pilietis, kadangi nepakanka dokumentų dokumentų G. A. Gochin ir Samuilo (Samuelio) Gochino giminystės ryšiui įrodyti (duotų pasų žinių lape nenurodyta Samuilo (Samuelio) Gochino gimimo data ir vieta), be to asmuo yra Jungtinių Amerikos Valstijų ir Pietų Afrikos pilietis.
2. Apie priimtą sprendimą pranešti G. A. Gochin.

Šis sprendimas gali būti skundžiamas Lietuvos Respublikos administracinių bylų teisenos įstatyme nustatyta tvarka.

Kopija tikra

Daiva Vežikauskaitė

Citizenship denial dated

June 18, 2007.

I had submitted the application. The Lithuanian Migration Department was required to respond every six months, which it did, requesting additional documents—apparently just general delaying tactics, as Breckinridge Long had done. The most-often requested document was Sam's birth certificate. The Ministry of the Interior was advised that those records had been destroyed on April 17, 1915, during the First World War, and the Lithuanian State Historical Archives verified the information in their document (PI-9652) P2-8908 dated September 4, 2007. Nonetheless, the Ministry of the Interior repeatedly requested the nonexistent birth record.

Two years after I submitted my application, on November 13, 2006, the Constitutional Court ruled that dual citizenship was to be limited. Initially there was confusion as to whether the ruling applied to cases currently under review, or only to cases that would be submitted in the future. It took a few months to clarify, and on June 18, 2007, the Lithuanian government was enabled to reach a decision.

Reason 1: Application denied due to insufficient proof.

Reason 2: Dual citizenship no longer allowed.

The decision was provided to me on July 18, 2007. There was a thirty-day appeal period, and the decision was issued to me on the thirtieth day, allowing zero days remaining to appeal.

This was the identical game they had played with my great-grandmother in 1922, except that in 1922, many, many of my relatives died as a result of governments' actions.

I recognized that the Lithuanian government of 1922 and the Lithuanian government of 2007 had remarkable parallels. Out of respect for my grandfather, I would not tolerate this reprehensible conduct. My great-grandmother, my grandfather, and all our families had been oppressed victims then, and decided that I would not allow repeated abuse. And so I responded.

Initially my agenda was to have my case heard in a court, where, I had hoped, an intelligent, independent, impartial judge would hear of the Migration Department's conduct and be as appalled as I was. Until that time, I had no idea that Lithuania had not changed in 100 years.

CASE #1

NUORAŠAS

Civiline byla Nr. 2-1396-553/08
Procesinio sprendimo kategorija:
117.1.;118.1.;

VILNIAUS MIESTO 2 APYLINKĖS TEISMAS

NUTARTIS
2008 m. vasario 25 d.
Vilnius

Vilniaus miesto 2 apylinkės teismo teisėja Aldona Tilindienė, sekretoriaujant Liucijai Vidžiūnienei, dalyvaujant pareiškėjo atstovei advokato padėjėjai Ievai Klimavičiūtei, viešame teismo posėdyje išnagrinėjo civilinę bylą pagal pareiškėjo Grant Arthur Gochin pareiškimą, dėl juridinę reikšmę turinčio fakto nustatymo suinteresuotam asmeniui Migracijos departamentui prie VRM,

n u s t a t ė:

Pareiškėjas kreipėsi į teismą prašydamas nustatyti juridinę reikšmę turintį faktą, kad Samuilis (Samuelis) Gochinas, pareiškėjo Grant Arthur Gochin, buvo Lietuvos Respublikos pilietis.

Pareiškėjas nurodo, kad jis siekia gauti Lietuvos Respublikos pilietybę, kadangi pareiškėjo senelis - Samuilis (Samuelas) Gochinas turėjo Lietuvos Respublikos pilietybę, tačiau šį faktą tiesiogiai patvirtinantys dokumentai nėra išlikę, todėl pareiškėjas yra priverstas kreiptis į teismą, siekdamas nustatyti juridinę reikšmę turintį faktą, kad Samuilis (Samuelis) Gochinas, pareiškėjo Grant Arthur Gochin senelis, buvo Lietuvos Respublikos pilietis. Pareiškėjas teismui nurodo, kad buvo atlikti genealoginiai pareiškėjo šeimos tyrimai įvairiuose Lietuvos archyvuose bei rasti dokumentai, patvirtinantys tai, kad Samuelis (Samuelis) Gochinas yra Grant Arthur Gochin senelis, tuatjje Lietuvos Respublikos pilietybę. Pareiškėjo Grant Arthur Gochin tėvas yra Harold Gochin, šį faktą patvirtina pateikiama pilna gimimo metrika bei jos vertimas. Harold Gochin tėvas buvo Lietuvos Respublikos pilietis Samuilis (Samuelas) Gochinas, gimęs Lietuvoje, šį faktą patvirtina pateikiama 1923 m. gimimo aktoNr. 17 informacija. Pareiškėjas taip pat nurodo, kad Grant Arthur Gochin senelis Samuilis (Samuelis) Gochinas gimė 1902 m. vasario 15 d. Papilėje, Lietuvoje (tuometinėje Kauno gubernijoje). Jo gimimas turėjo būti įregistruotas Papilės žydų bendruomenės metrikų knygose, tačiau Lietuvos valstybės istorijos archyvo 2007 m. rugsėjo 4 d. rašte Nr. (P1-9652)P2-8908, nurodoma, kad nėra išlikę Papilės žydų bendruomenės 1900-1905 metų metrikų knygų, todėl nėra galimybės išduoti archyvo pažymos apie Samuilio (Samuelio) Gochin gimimą. Yra žinoma, kad I Pasaulinio karo pabaigoje S. Gochinas kartu su savo šeima atsidūrė Charkove (Ukrainoje), iš kur 1922 m. pabaigoje grįžo ir vėl apsigyveno Papilėje. Šiaulių miesto ir apskrities viršininko fonde neišliko ir dokumentai, susiję su Šiaulių naujokų ėmimo komisijos veikla. Kreipusis į Lietuvos centrinį valstybės archyvą buvo gauti išlikę dokumentai. Yra išlikusi Šiaulių miesto ir apskrities viršininko byla Nr. 53 -, kurioje pateikiami 1926 m. sausio, vasario ir kovo mėnesių vidaus pasų žinių lapai. Minėtoje byloje Šiaulių apskrities Papilės valsčiaus pasų žinių lape yra nurodoma, kad 1926 m. sausio 15 d. Samuilui (Samueliui) Gochinui, gimusiam Papilėje, buvo išduotas Lietuvos Respublikos vidaus pasas (pasų knygų eilės Nr. 4306). Pareiškėjas pažymi, kad Samuilio (Samuelio) Gochino Lietuvos Respublikos vidaus pasas nėra išlikęs. 1926 m. kovą S.Gochinas išvyko į Pietų

Court Decision dated February 25, 2008.

This case was heard by one judge at Vilnius City 2nd District Court.[32]

---

[32]Civiline byla Nr. 2-1396-553/08. Procesinio sprendimo kategorija:

The court confirmed that the Papile vital records had not survived WWI.

Vice-dean from humanities faculty at Vytautas Magnus University, Lithuanian War History Association chairman, and Associate Professor Dr. Jonis Vaicenonis testified that he had viewed my grandfather's photographs, identified his unit, and from that evidence was able to find my grandfather's military records. The professor testified that there was absolutely no question of my grandfather's Lithuanian citizenship.

In "Military Compulsory Service Law," published in *Vyriausybes zinios* (Administration News), (Kaunas, June 3, 1922, Nr. 91), the first article declares: "every male citizen of Lithuania must complete compulsory military service," which serves as legal confirmation that to have been in the Lithuanian military, my grandfather had to have been a Lithuanian citizen.

The court rejected this testimony, asserting that the photograph shown to the professor could have been of anybody, and that because Samuel Gochin's military records had been found did not prove any relationship to me, i.e., it was possible we had found the unrelated Samuel Gochin's records, a photo of somebody in that uniform of that military unit, and claimed that it was my grandfather, and therefore, both the professor (whom I had never met previously) and me, were lying. One must admit there is creativity in that means of disposing of evidence! The government then required a "portraiture investigation" into the photographs, but did not detail what that investigation might involve. It was obviously a ridiculous attempt to deny objective evidence, a requirement request that could not be met.

Professor Bendikaite of Vilnius University also offered testimony, but it too was rejected.

117.1.;118.1.

The court also said that as I already have South African and American citizenships, the application was void, which is in contravention of their own citizenship law. According to the law, I would be given a choice of citizenships to take. Instead, the Lithuanian government and courts had made the decision for me, without asking for my response. This was a straightforward denial of a right under their law, but consistent with the existing perception of denying Jewish citizenship in order to avoid the possibility of property claims.

The court ruled that there had been a citizen of Lithuania named Samuel Gochin, but found no relationship between that Samuel Gochin and me, and dismissed my case.

I appealed this incomprehensible decision to a higher court.

CASE #2

Administracinė byla Nr. I-2369-426/2008
Procesinio sprendimo kategorija 3.5; 74

VILNIAUS APYGARDOS ADMINISTRACINIS TEISMAS

SPRENDIMAS
LIETUVOS RESPUBLIKOS VARDU

2008 m. rugsėjo 18 d.
Vilnius

Vilniaus apygardos administracinio teismo teisėjų kolegija, susidedanti iš teisėjų Henriko Sadausko (kolegijos pirmininkas), Ritos Miliuvienės (pranešėja) ir Raimondo Blauzdžiūno, sekretoriaujant Aurelijai Pauliukaitei, dalyvaujant pareiškėjo atstovei advokato padėjėjai Ievai Klimavičiūtei, atsakovo atstovei Ramūnei Žukļjaitei, viešame teismo posėdyje išnagrinėjo administracinę bylą pagal pareiškėjo Grant Arthur Gochin skundą dėl Migracijos departamento prie Lietuvos Respublikos vidaus reikalų ministerijos sprendimo panaikinimo ir įpareigojimo atlikti veiksmus.

Teisėjų kolegija, išnagrinėjusi bylą,

n u s t a t ė :

pareiškėjas Grant Arthur Gochin prašo panaikinti Migracijos departamento prie Vidaus reikalų ministerijos 2007 m. birželio 18 d sprendimą Nr. (15/3-11)8P-675 ir įpareigoti atsakovą iš naujo spręsti pareiškėjo Lietuvos Respublikos pilietybės klausimą.

Skunde (b. l. 3-7) pasiūkino, kad jo tėvas yra Harold Gochin. Šį faktą patvirtina pateikiama pilna gimimo metrika bei jos vertinimas. Pastarojo tėvas buvo Lietuvos Respublikos pilietis Samuilis (Samuelis) Gochinas, gimęs Lietuvoje. Šį faktą patvirtina pateikiama 1923 m. gimimo akto Nr. 17 informacija. Kadangi jo senelis turėjo Lietuvos Respublikos pilietybę, pareiškėjas kreipėsi į Migracijos departamentą su prašymu spręsti jo pilietybės klausimą. Manu, kad Migracijos departamentas nepagrįstai atmetė jo prašymą. Atlikti genealoginiai įeismu tyrimai įvairiuose Lietuvos archyvuose bei rasti dokumentai patvirtina tai, kad Samuelis Gochinas yra Grant Arthur Gochin senelis, turėjęs Lietuvos Respublikos pilietybę. Migracijos departamentui kartu su prašymu buvo pateikti visi turimi dokumentai, įrodantys šį faktą. Pareiškėjo nuomone, ginčijamas sprendimas yra nepagrįstas, nemotyvuotas, neatitinkantis teisinio reguliavimo bei protingumo ir sąžiningumo principų, todėl turi būti panaikintas.

Tvirtina, kad Samuilis (Samuelis) Gochinas gimė 1902 m. vasario 15 d. Papilėje, Lietuvoje (buvometinėje Kauno gubernijoje). Jo gimimas turėjo būti įregistruotas Papilės žydų bendruomenės metrikų knygose, tačiau įrašo iš šių knygų apie jo gimimo vieta ir laiką nėra galimybės pateikti dėl objektyvių, nuo pareiškėjo valios nepriklausančių priežasčių - Papilės žydų bendruomenės metrikų knygos iš XX a. pr. prašuvo dar Pirmojo pasaulinio karo metu. Per Pirmąjį pasaulinį karą Samuilis (Samuelis) Gochinas kartu su savo šeima, kaip ir daugelis Lietuvos žydų, caro karinės valdžios buvo ištremtas iš savo gimtųjų vietų į Rusijos imperijos gilumą. Yra žinoma, kad Pirmojo pasaulinio karo pabaigoje šeima atsidūrė Charkove (Ukrainoje), iš kur 1922 m. pabaigoje grįžo ir vėl apsigyveno Papilėje. Daug medžiagos neišliko dėl Antrojo pasaulinio karo ir jo padarinių. Šiaulių miesto ir apskrities viršininko fonde neišliko

[signature] **KOPIJA TIKRA**

Court Decision dated September 18, 2008.

At Vilnius Regional AdministrativeCourt[33]

This was a three-judge panel, which meant that now four of Lithuania's judges had adjudicated my case.

---

[33] Administracine byla Nr. I-2369-426/2008. Procesinio sprendimo kategorija 3.5; 74

The Lithuanian Ministry of the Interior again defended their position in court, stating that the Lithuanian internal passport data did not contain dates of birth, and that the one and only document they would accept, which would prove to them that Sam was my grandfather, was his birth certificate, i.e. the single document they knew with certainty could not be produced.

This court re-affirmed the lower court's decision.

The government postulated a theory that there could have been two Samuel Gochins, both born in Papile, of the same age, and that while I was certainly related to *a* Samuel Gochin, I was unable to prove whether I was related to the Samuel Gochin in the documents or the Samuel Gochin of their imagination.

The available population figure for Papile in the year closest to Sam's birth was 1897. On that date, Papile had 1877 people, of which 965 were Jews.[34] So among those 965 Jews, according to the Lithuanian government, there could have been two families with the same names, both giving birth to a son on the same date, both naming their sons Sam, and only one of those families registering the birth. I couldn't prove which of the Sam's was my grandfather. It was crystal clear to the three Lithuanian judges who were hearing this case that I had not proved to be Sam's grandson. Franz Kafka could not have created a more ridiculous scenario: the impossible task of having to prove a negative. This was a creative judicial finding to accommodate a governmental ruling, the very definition of a kangaroo court. Strangely enough, this court declared that they had exercised "complete, thorough, and objective analysis," using the criteria of "justice and intelligence." Clearly Soviet-era justice and intelligence in modern-day independent Lithuania!

There is a rule in Lithuania that if three Lithuanian citizens offer testimonials of someone else's Lithuanian citizenship, that by itself is

---

[34]http://www.jewishgen.org/yizkor/pinkas_lita/lit_00470.html

sufficient proof of citizenship. I obtained three such testimonies. One of those testimonies was from my aunt Esther Barsel, who was born in Raguva, in Lithuania. Esther was one of Nelson Mandela's best friends; she is one of South Africa's national heroes who fought for that country's liberation. Liberia posthumously issued a postage stamp to honor her as a "Legendary Hero of Africa." Her husband, Hymie Barsel, also a Litvak, was also a South African national hero, and also had a national postage stamp issued in his honor.

The Lithuanian Migration Department claimed that none of those offering sworn testimony, including Esther, could have been in attendance at my grandfather's birth, and therefore could not determine whether a man they had known their entire lives might have been lying about his place of birth. This was again a very creative means of applying a *judenrein* legal interpretation. The three-judge court ruled that my relative's testimony was to be ascribed no credibility. (We all know that part of European history in which Jewish testimony had no weight in court.)

Testimony from Dr. Bendikaite of Vilnius University was again dismissed because she couldn't prove I was my grandfather's grandson.

At this point I knew with complete clarity that decisions in Lithuanian courts were predetermined, and that no testimony mattered.

Principle and human dignity are not usually matters to be adjudicated in a court, however I was so angry that these people could be so incredibly insulting to my relatives, that I was determined to take my case further. To me this was a clear example of a government and court ruling based on one word on an application: Jew. The year was 2008; it was no longer tolerable in an EU country.

Dual citizenship was now no longer allowed, and my case had no further legal basis on which to proceed. I was at a dead end.

I developed a new respect and admiration for Lithuanians—respect based on an incredible ability to be creative with legal evidence, and admiration for the time, effort, and expense they would expend to implement denial of Jewish citizenship applications. The cost of pursuing respect for my grandfather was worth more to me than the cost of litigation.

On June 22, 2009, I submitted a new application for a certificate called a Right of Retention to Lithuanian Citizenship.

The law on citizenship provides for the "retention" of the "right to citizenship" for persons (and their children, grandchildren, and great-grandchildren) who had previously resided in Lithuania but who are now living abroad. The retention policy was incorporated to allow former residents the ability to maintain their bond with Lithuania so that they would "not be severed from the Lithuanian nation." The certificate is a legal document which would declare only that Samuel Gochin was a Lithuanian citizen and my grandfather, but would not grant citizenship or any rights.

I simply wanted an admission from the government of Lithuania that my grandfather was Samuel Gochin, a Jew and a Lithuanian, and that these two identifiers were not mutually exclusive.

In order for me to apply for this certificate, I was required to offer additional proof for Lithuanian government consideration. I offered my uncle's birth certificate, showing that he was also a son of Samuel Gochin, who was born in Lithuania, and I offered my grandfather's death certificate, showing his place of birth as Lithuania.

DENIAL OF RIGHT OF RETENTION APPLICATION

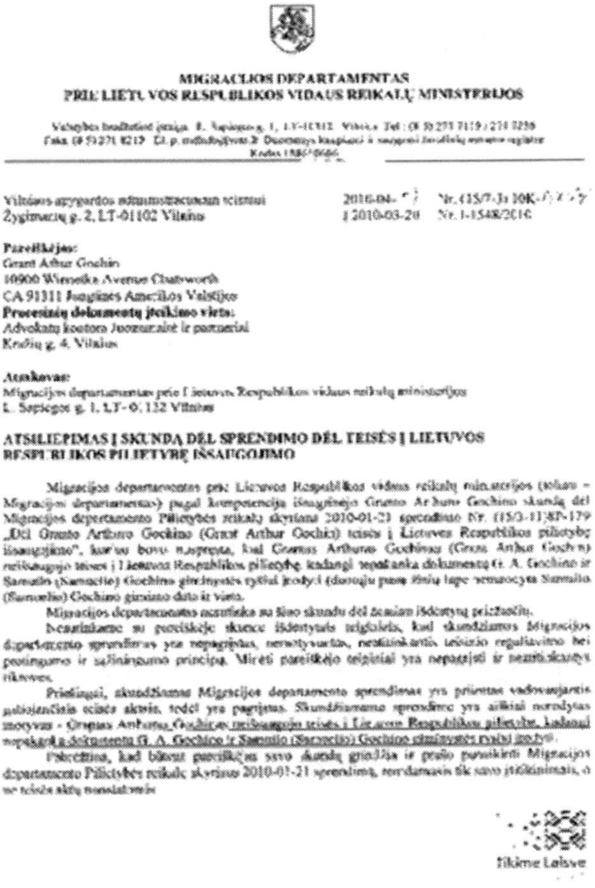

MIGRACIJOS DEPARTAMENTAS
PRIE LIETUVOS RESPUBLIKOS VIDAUS REIKALŲ MINISTERIJOS

[illegible]

Vilniaus apygardos administraciniam teismui
Žygimantų g. 2, LT-01102 Vilnius

[illegible]

Pareiškėjas:
Grant Arthur Gochin
10900 [illegible] Avenue Chatsworth
CA 91311 Jungtinės Amerikos Valstijos
Procesinių dokumentų įteikimo vieta:
Advokatų kontora [illegible] ir partneriai
Kražių g. 4, Vilnius

Atsakovas:
Migracijos departamentas prie Lietuvos Respublikos vidaus reikalų ministerijos
L. Sapiegos g. 1, LT-[illegible] Vilnius

ATSILIEPIMAS Į SKUNDĄ DĖL SPRENDIMO DĖL TEISĖS Į LIETUVOS RESPUBLIKOS PILIETYBĘ IŠSAUGOJIMO

[illegible]

Denial decision dated January 21, 2010

Whereas the Lithuanian government had taken almost three years to deny my citizenship application, this time they took only seven months to deny the Right of Retention application.

I now had a new basis with which to litigate against the Lithuanian government, and so I did.

CASE #3

Administracinė byla Nr. I-1548-171/2010
Procesо Nr. 3-61-3-00719-2010-3...
Procesinio sprendimo kategorija 3.5; 74

VILNIAUS APYGARDOS ADMINISTRACINIS TEISMAS
SPRENDIMAS
LIETUVOS RESPUBLIKOS VARDU
2010 m. rugsėjo 23 d.
Vilnius

Vilniaus apygardos administracinio teismo teisėjų kolegija, susidedanti iš teisėjų Irenos Paulauskienės (kolegijos pirmininkė ir pranešėja), Halinos Zaicevacienės ir Ernesto Spruogio, sekretoriaujant Jolntai Domarkaitei, dalyvaujant pareiškėjo atstovei advokatei padėjėjai Ievai Klimavičiūtei, atsakovo atstovei Ramonei Žukiljaitei,

viešame teismo posėdyje išnagrinėjo administracinę bylą pagal pareiškėjo Granto Arturo Gochino (Grant Arthur Gochin) skundą atsakovui Migracijos departamentui prie Lietuvos Respublikos vidaus reikalų ministerijos dėl sprendimo panaikinimo ir įpareigojimo atlikti veiksmus.

Teisėjų kolegija, išnagrinėjusi bylą,

nustatė:

pareiškėjas Grantas Arturas Gochinas pateikė teismui skundą (b. l. 3–5), kuriuo prašo:
1. panaikinti Migracijos departamento prie Vidaus reikalų ministerijos 2010 m. kovo 21 d sprendimą Nr. (15/3-11)8P-179;
2. įpareigoti atsakovą iš naujo spręsti pareiškėjo Lietuvos Respublikos pilietybės klausimą.

Paaiškino, kad 2009 m. birželio 22 d. pareiškėjas Grantas Arturas Gochinas, vadovaudamasis Pilietybės įstatymo 17 straipsniu, kreipėsi į atsakovą su prašymu išduoti teisės į Lietuvos Respublikos pilietybę išsaugojimo patvirtinimą, kadangi pareiškėjo senelis Samuelis (Samuel) Gochinas, 1901 m. gimęs Lietuvoje, iki 1940 m. birželio 15 d. turėjo Lietuvos pilietybę.

Nurodo, kad pareiškėjas pagrįstai kreipėsi į atsakovą su prašymu spręsti jo Lietuvos Respublikos pilietybės išsaugojimo klausimą, nurodydamas, kad jo senelis iki 1940 m. birželio 15 d. turėjo Lietuvos pilietybę. Migracijos departamentas visiškai nepagrįstai pripažino pareiškėjo pateiktus dokumentus nepatikimais giminystės ryšiui įrodyti, todėl pareiškėjo prašymą atmetė.

Pažymėjo, jog šioje byloje nėra ginčo dėl to ar pareiškėjo senelis Samuelis (Samuelis) Gochinas turėjo Lietuvos Respublikos pilietybę, kadangi atsakovas iš fakta pripažino. Ginčo y nor šioje apygardos klausimas, ar pagrįstai atsakovas atmetė pareiškėjo prašymą dėl Lietuvos Respublikos pilietybės išsaugojimo, remdamasis argumentu, esą negalaima dokumenų pareiškėjo ir jo senelio Samuelio (Samuelio) Gochino giminystės ryšiui įrodyti (duotųjų pasų žinių bpo neatitinka Samuelio (Samuelio) Gochino gimimo data ir vieta).

Skunde nurodo, kad pareiškėjo Granto Arturo Gochino tėvas yra Haroldas Gochinas (Harold Gochin). Ji pateikiamo Pietų Afrikos Respublikos Skuodo pilnas gimimo rotrikos bei jos vertimo matyti, kad pareiškėjas gimė 1965 m. kapkricio 2 d., Port Elisabeth, Haroldo Gochino ir Sandros Jean Smolkan (mergautinė pavarde) šeimoje. Haroldo Gochino tėvas (pareiškėjo senelis) buvo Lietuvos Respublikos pilietis Samuelis (Samuel) Gochinas, gimęs Lietuvoje. Tai patvirtina patcikiamas Haroldo Gochino gimimo liudijimo vertikas bei 1925 m. gimimo akto Nr. 17 informacija. Iš kurios matyti, kad 1953 m. birželio 13 d. Samuelio Gochino ir jo žmonos Doros Rummel šeimoje, Port Elisabeth, Pietų Afrikos Respublikoje, gimė sūnus (pareiškėjo tėvas), kuriam buvo duotas Haroldo vardas.

Court Decision dated September 23, 2010

At Vilnius Regional Administrative Court [35]

---

[35]Administracine byla Nr. I-2369-426/2008. Procesinio sprendimo

This was also a three-judge panel, which meant that now seven of Lithuania's judges had adjudicated my case.

In previous cases, the Lithuanian government claimed that the lack of my grandfather's birth record made it impossible for me to prove that he was my grandfather, and to them, South African records did not prove he was the Samuel Gochin of the Lithuanian records. According to the Lithuanian government, in 1933, when my father was born, my grandfather may have had reason to lie about where he was born. And so, like the other 90 percent of South African Jews originating in Lithuania, he could have falsely stated that he was born in Lithuania.

Harold's (my father's) South African birth certificate showed that his father, Samuel Gochin, age 31, was born in Lithuania. This offers a possible date range for Sam's Birth of June 14, 1901 to June 12, 1903. Sam's South African national identification number identified his date of birth as February 15, 1902. The Papile Jewish Community had used a date of December 26, 1902.

When Sam died, the mortuary collected his body and filed his death certificate. Instead of showing his birth as February 15, 1902, the mortuary made a typographical error, reflecting his date of birth as February 15, 1901. A simple error, easily explained, especially given the overwhelming amount of evidence provided. But at this point we know with clarity that Lithuania will not recognize this Jew, me, as the grandson of Sam—they finally had one item that showed a conflict. The date of birth stated by the mortuary was 119 days different than that which was shown on my father's birth certificate. This, from an era in which dates of birth were seldom, if ever, reflected accurately.

Rational thought would indicate: a tiny village, Sam's parents had the same names, the rabbinical records reflected his birth, the letters of testimony, two Lithuanian professors testified, military records, internal

kategorija 3.5; 74

passport records, South African government records. The records were consistent across two continents and 100 years, except for one date that was reported by a non-family member who had never met Sam. Given the weight of the evidence versus a small clerical error, how would one think this should be adjudicated?

The case was dismissed by the court. My next step—the Lithuanian Supreme Court.

LITHUANIA'S "TRUMP CARD"

Sam's South African Death Certificate.

The Lithuanian Government finally had something to validate their declination.

CASE #4

Administracines byla Nr. A⁸²²-2124/2011
Teisminio proceso Nr. 3-61-3-00719-2010-3
Procesinio sprendimo kategorijos: 3.5; 79.1.

LIETUVOS VYRIAUSIASIS ADMINISTRACINIS TEISMAS

SPRENDIMAS
LIETUVOS RESPUBLIKOS VARDU

2011 m. liepos 21 d.
Vilnius

Lietuvos vyriausiojo administracinio teismo teisėjų kolegija, susidedanti iš teisėjų Audriaus Bakavecko, Dainiaus Raižio (kolegijos pirmininkas) ir Skirgailės Žalimienės (pranešėja), sekretoriaujant Lilijai Andrijauskaitei,

dalyvaujant pareiškėjo Granto Arturo Gochino (Grant Arthur Gochin) atstovei Laurai Altun, atsakovo Migracijos departamento prie Lietuvos Respublikos vidaus reikalų ministerijos atstovei Agnei Urnavičienei,

viešame teismo posėdyje apeliacinio proceso tvarka išnagrinėjo administracinę bylą pagal pareiškėjo Granto Arturo Gochino (Grant Arthur Gochin) apeliacinį skundą dėl Vilniaus apygardos administracinio teismo 2010 m. rugsėjo 23 d. sprendimo administracinėje byloje pagal pareiškėjo Granto Arturo Gochino skundą atsakovui Migracijos departamentui prie Lietuvos Respublikos vidaus reikalų ministerijos dėl sprendimo panaikinimo ir įpareigojimo atlikti veiksmus.

Teisėjų kolegija

n u s t a t ė:

I.

Pareiškėjas Grantas Arturas Gochinas (toliau – ir pareiškėjas) pateikė teismui skundą (b. l. 1–5), kuriuo prašė: 1) panaikinti Migracijos departamento prie Lietuvos Respublikos vidaus reikalų ministerijos (toliau – ir atsakovas, Migracijos departamentas) 2010 m. sausio 21 d. sprendimą Nr. (15/2-11)4P-179 (toliau – ir Sprendimas); 2) įpareigoti Migracijos departamentą iš naujo spręsti pareiškėjo teisės į Lietuvos Respublikos pilietybę išsaugojimo klausimą ir priimti sprendimą dėl Grant Arthur Gochin teisės į Lietuvos Respublikos pilietybę išsaugojimo pagal Pilietybės įstatymo 17 straipsnio 1 dalį kaip asmens iki 1940 m. birželio 15 d. turėjusio Lietuvos pilietybę, vaikaičiui gyvenančiam kitoje valstybėje, o būtent kaip Samuilio (Samuelio) Gochino anūkui Grant Arthur Gochin, gimusiam 1963 m. lapkričio 2 d. Pietų Afrikos Respublikoje, Port Elizabeth.

Pareiškėjas nurodė, jog 2009 m. birželio 22 d. jis, vadovaudamasis Pilietybės įstatymo 17 straipsnio, kreipėsi į atsakovą su prašymu išduoti teisės į Lietuvos Respublikos pilietybę išsaugojimo pažymėjimą, kadangi pareiškėjo senelis Samuilis (Samuel) Gochinas iki 1940 m. birželio 15 d. turėjo Lietuvos pilietybę. Nurodo, kad Migracijos departamentas visiškai nepagrįstai pripažino pareiškėjo pateiktus dokumentus nepakankamais giminystės ryšiui įrodyti ir pareiškėjo prašymą atmetė.

Pareiškėjas pažymėjo, jog šioje byloje nėra ginčo dėl to, ar pareiškėjo senelis Samuilis (Samuelis) Gochinas turėjo Lietuvos Respublikos pilietybę, kadangi atsakovas šį faktą pripažino. Svarbiausias klausimas, ar pagrįstai atsakovas atmetė pareiškėjo prašymą dėl Lietuvos Respublikos pilietybės išsaugojimo, remdamasis argumentu, esą nepakanka duomenų, pareiškėjo ir jo senelio Samuilio (Samuelio) Gochino giminystės ryšiui įrodyti (duotųjų pačų žinių lape samurodyta Samuilis

At Lithuanian Supreme Administrative Court[36]

Three-judge panel, which brings it to ten Lithuanian judges who had

---

[36]Administracine byla Nr. A822-2124/2011.Teisminio proceso Nr. 3-61-3-00719-2010-3. Procesinio sprendimo kategorija 3.5; 79.1

now adjudicated my case.

I had no expectation that anything would change at the Supreme Court of Lithuania. I viewed this case as a stepping-stone to move my case to the European Union Court of Human Rights at Strasbourg. However circumstances changed.

On June 22, 2011,[37] the Lithuanian Parliament passed a bill that will allow for minimal repayments to the Jewish community for properties that were seized around the time of WW2. The subject of property restitution was now finally closed.

Just as the Supreme Court case of 2006 on the permissibility of Lithuanian dual citizenship had enabled the Migration Department to issue me a citizenship denial, this restitution settlement now enabled the courts to actually adjudicate my case.

The Migration Department of Lithuania defended their case, claiming that I had "deceitfully" misled the court by offering misleading facts. These misleading facts were, apparently:

- I had claimed that Sam Gochin was born in Papile, when the internal passports had reflected that he had merely lived there.
- I was deceitful in stating that the Papile records had been destroyed (as they had been officially advised by the Lithuanian archives). They posed that it could be possible that the archives still existed in some yet-to-be-found unknown locale.

The High Administrative Court (Supreme Court) issued their ruling on July 21, 2011, and found it inconceivable that the lower courts could not find that Sam Gochin was my grandfather. They ruled that the lower courts had not adjudicated the facts, and had not provided reasons for rejecting the documentary proof in the case. They found the lower courts' and Migration Department's decisions "unjust and wrongly

---

[37] http://www.baltictimes.com/news/articles/28927/

motivated," and declared that my Sam Gochin was indeed my grandfather and a Lithuanian citizen. A six-and-a-half year legal battle to have my grandfather recognized as a Lithuanian citizen had, at long last, succeeded. The Lithuanian government had now defended four legal actions. The amount of time and resources they devoted to denying the application of one Jew is inexplicable, especially when their own Supreme Court recognized the government's arguments as "absurd" and "inconceivable."

The single difference between this case and the previous cases is that now the matter of property restitution had been settled and was closed.

As an example of the restitution agreed upon by the Lithuanian government, in 2013, 870,000 euros will be granted by the Lithuanian government to be divided between approximately 2000 survivors.

For thirteen years, negotiators negotiated with the Lithuanian government about getting back communal property. As an example in Kaunas alone, two Hebrew high schools alone (in prime locations)—beautiful buildings—are probably worth 50–60 million euros. Add the hospital, the sports club, additional schools, orphanages, elderly people's home, Zionist institutions, and much more—all built with Jewish money and once belonging to the Jewish community, religious and not religious. This does not address privately owned Jewish property. The total restitution amount over a ten-year period will be about $50,000,000, and much of that will be allocated to "joint" government projects, i.e. building Jewish tourist facilities to bring fresh Jewish tourism dollars to present-day Lithuania.

CASE #5

Decision dated September 26, 2011

At Vilnius Regional Administrative Court[38]

Three-judge panel. This brings it to thirteen Lithuanian judges who had adjudicated my case.

I brought an action against the Lithuanian government, in their courts,

---

[38]Administracine byla Nr. I=1548-171/2010. Teisminio proceso Nr. 3-61-3-00719-2010-3. Procesinio sprendimo kategorija 59; 73.

to force them to reimburse my legal fees. I won partial reimbursement. These reimbursement funds were immediately donated to *www.survivormitzvah.org* to assist needy Holocaust victims still remaining behind in Lithuania.

RIGHT OF RETENTION ISSUED

MIGRACIJOS DEPARTAMENTAS
PRIE LIETUVOS RESPUBLIKOS VIDAUS REIKALŲ MINISTERIJOS

SPRENDIMAS
DĖL GRANTO ARTHURO GOCHINO (GRANT ARTHUR GOCHIN) TEISĖS Į
LIETUVOS RESPUBLIKOS PILIETYBĘ IŠSAUGOJIMO

2011 m. spalio 26 d. Nr. (15/3-11) 8P-1340
Vilnius

Migracijos departamentas prie Vidaus reikalų ministerijos išnagrinėjo Granto Arthuro Gochino (Grant Arthur Gochin) prašymą ir dokumentus dėl teisės į Lietuvos Respublikos pilietybę išsaugojimo.

Grantas Arthuras Gochinas (Grant Arthur Gochin) gimė 1963-11-02 Pietų Afrikos Respublikoje, Port Elisabeth. Asmuo gyvena Jungtinėse Amerikos Valstijose. G. A. Gochinas yra Jungtinių Amerikos Valstijų ir Pietų Afrikos pilietis – atsižinkamai tai patvirtina Jungtinių Amerikos Valstijų piliečio pasas Nr. 038735574, išduotas 2004-02-10 Los Andželo pasų agentūros, ir Pietų Afrikos Respublikos piliečio pasas Nr. 403265718, išduotas 1997-02-11 Vidaus reikalų ministerijos (šio paso galiojimas baigėsi 2007-02-10).

2011-08-08 Migracijos departamente prie Vidaus reikalų ministerijos buvo gautas Lietuvos vyriausiojo administracinio teismo 2011-07-21 sprendimas, kuriuo nuspręsta pareiškėjo G. A. Gochino apeliacinį skundą patenkinti iš dalies, Vilniaus apygardos administracinio teismo 2010-09-23 sprendimą panaikinti ir priimti naują sprendimą: pareiškėjo G. A. Gochino skundą patenkinti ir panaikinti Migracijos departamento prie Vidaus reikalų ministerijos 2010-01-21 sprendimą Nr. (15/3-11) 8P-179 bei įpareigoti Migracijos departamentą prie Vidaus reikalų ministerijos iš naujo išnagrinėti G. A. Gochino prašymą dėl teisės į Lietuvos Respublikos pilietybę išsaugojimo. Šiame Lietuvos vyriausiojo administracinio teismo 2011-07-21 sprendime suponuota išvada, kad Samuilis (Samelis) Gochinas gimė 1902-02-15, ir teisėjų kolegija padarė išvadą, jog tikėtina išvada yra tai, kad pareiškėjas yra Samuilio (Samuelio) Gochino vaikaitis. Be to, Šiaulių m. ir apsk. viršininko pasų skyrius byloje Nr. 37 „Žinios apie išduotus vidaus pasus Papilės valsčiaus valdybos" įrašyta, kad 1924-11-05 Samuilui Gochinui išduotas pasas Nr. 767121.

Vadovaudamasis Lietuvos Respublikos pilietybės įstatymo (Žin., 2010, Nr. 144-7361) 45 straipsnio 5 dalimi, Lietuvos Respublikos pilietybės įstatymo (Žin., 2002, Nr. 95-4087; 2008, Nr. 83-3293) 17 straipsnio 1 dalies 1 punktu, 22 straipsnio 4 dalimi, 24 straipsnio 4 dalimi, 28 straipsnio 1 dalimi, Lietuvos Respublikos vidaus reikalų ministro 2011 m. gegužės 16 d. įsakymo Nr. 1V-377 „Dėl įgaliojimų suteikimo" (Žin., 2011, Nr. 61-2920) 1.1.1. punktu ir atsižvelgdamas į Lietuvos vyriausiojo administracinio teismo 2011-07-21 sprendimą bei pateiktus dokumentus,

n u s p r e n d ž i u, kad:
1. Grantas Arthuras Gochinas (Grant Arthur Gochin), gim. 1963-11-02 Pietų Afrikos Respublikoje, Port Elisabeth, išsaugo teisę į Lietuvos Respublikos pilietybę kaip asmens, iki 1940-06-15 turėjusio Lietuvos pilietybę, vaikaitis, gyvenantis kitoje valstybėje.
2. Apie priimtą sprendimą turi būti pranešta G. A. Gochinui.

Šis sprendimas gali būti skundžiamas įstatymų nustatyta tvarka Administracinių ginčų komisijai arba administraciniam teismui.

Direktorius   Almantas Gavėnas

Certificate of Right of Retention to Lithuanian Citizenship:

October 26, 2011

On October 26, 2011, the Lithuanian government issued a new finding that Samuel Gochin was my grandfather, and a Lithuanian citizen. My grandfather now again existed as a legally recognized Jewish Lithuanian man, it was the respect he so richly deserved.

There was no property under question in this claim; it was an emotional quest only. Imagine their fight if there had been assets to claim!

The Lithuanian government will tell you that they mourn their murdered Jews; one wonders if it is only living Jews they don't particularly like. The Lithuanian government seeks investment and tourism from the descendants of their Litvak Jewish population, but here is a case that traveled through five courts in Lithuania, viewed by a total of thirteen judges, adjudicated by an untold number of government departments, and the conduct at the highest levels of government shows one and only one intent. You can determine that intent yourself. Is that the same intent shown by their diplomats who mourn for Lithuanian Jews while they are outside the country, and while in front of Jewish audiences, but do not echo those same sentiments when they are back home in Vilnius? Certainly, the Interior Ministry did not share those sentiments, but the closure of the restitution law in 2011, and the now desperate need they share for Jewish assets, may well have changed their most insincere statements. When their foreign ministry speaks of meeting Litvaks all over the world, having the government also view them as Litvaks is dependent upon the timing of restitution law, so no statement, from any Lithuanian government official may ever be accepted at face value, knowing their disingenuity when there was ever a possibility of a property claim.

For Jews who are attracted to Lithuania for investment purposes as suggested by the government—if there is an absence of a legal system, or if there is a legal system that issues decisions that are predetermined based on whether or not somebody is a Jew, is that somewhere you would want to invest? Lithuanian courts are kangaroo courts; would a prudent business entrust its affairs to such a system?

When the government repeatedly honors Jew murderers and withholds pensions from those who rescued Jews,[39] is this a country where one wants to spend tourism time and money?

Regarding my legal case, the Lithuanian government did not have to re-invent a strategy; they already had it in place. While they employed the very same strategy with my great-grandmother Chaie in 1922, she was defenseless, and many, many relatives died as a result. This time I was not defenseless, so the game had changed.

The Lithuanian Ministry of Foreign Affairs will tell you that there is not a "Jewish" aspect to all of these cases. I have laid out the facts and ask that you come to your own conclusion. Lithuanian officials acknowledge that they have a "bad past" but that it is different now. My final case was heard in 2011, so how different is their past to their present? In a visit to Israel in May 2013, the Lithuanian prime minister announced with pride that since they changed their citizenship law in 2011, more than 4000 Israelis have been granted Lithuanian citizenship. Apparently, for Lithuania, history begins in 2011.[40]

Lithuania, which has a population of around 3.2 million, has seen about 700,000 people leave the country since its independence twenty years ago. Today Lithuania NEEDS citizens, they NEED foreign investment, and they NEED foreign tourism. With the closure of restitution issues in 2011, their perceived best target is to cater to descendant Litvaks, offering platitudes and fake grief, in order to meet their own needs. Malice, murder, manipulation, and honoring of murderers should have no term limits; Jewish survival has required long-term memory. Let us not forget those that were murdered at the hands of those that Lithuania considers her national heroes.

These cases prove one point: one person can stand against a national

---

[39] http://www.lithuaniatribune.com/13470/no-money-for-the-jew-rescuers-201213470

[40] http://www.jpost.com/National-News/Lithuanian-FM-to-Israel-Heed-settlement-goods-label-issue-313937

government and require truth. My accomplishment here is that I have honored my grandfather and his dignity, and forced a dishonest government and court system to tell the truth.

MULTIPLE CITIZENSHIP

Holding multiple citizenships is an insurance policy. If our ancestors had multiple citizenship, they could have left Lithuania, Germany, or Poland and moved without bureaucracy to the country of their alternate citizenship. Foreign citizenship was and still is a form of an insurance policy, only far cheaper and more effective than any insurance policy that could be purchased. Genocide would never take place if the victims held two passports.

One-third of all Americans have passports. Can anybody think of even one Jewish-American who does not have a passport?

Almost every Israeli citizen has a passport, and many of them have multiple passports from different countries. This is a benefit to Israel and the Jewish people as a whole. In order for the Jewish people to grow, Jews need to survive first, and a second passport is a means to survival.

In a world that distinguishes between Jews and non-Jews, between one nationality or another, multiple citizenships are passports to safety. Some items to contemplate as we progress:

In April 2013, Chechen terrorists attacked Boston. The younger terrorist did not murder a driver because he was <u>not</u> American. A foreign passport can be a lifesaver.

In the terrorist attacks in Mumbai, in November 2008, those terrorists told Americans and Britons to go one way, and all other citizens were allowed to leave.

In the case of Leon Klinghoffer on the Achille Lauro, in 1985, Palestinian terrorists threw an American Jew overboard and drowned him for being American and Jewish.

Who believes that Gilad Shalit would have been spared by his abducting terrorists had he only held Israeli citizenship? He held dual Israeli and French citizenship. The French government interceded and negotiated for his life. His French passport likely determined his survival.

These are simply a few examples of Jews going about daily life, vacationing and living, and being murdered for who they are. A foreign citizenship in all those cases may have saved their lives. Is it too much cost and effort to provide additional documents for our next generations to offer one added layer of safety?

Rights to heritage citizenship reclamations will go away in the next generation; this is our final opportunity to make our family heritage statements.

Very few Jews exist in Europe. As our children go on the "March of the Living," claiming heritage citizenship is also a means of stating, "You did not kill all of us." As rights are retained and passed to future generations, the names of our ancestors will be remembered, thus ensuring their immortality in the form of the Talmudic statement that as long as somebody's name is mentioned and recalled, they are not truly dead.

European citizenship was a liability to our ancestors; it is a benefit to us today.

Dual citizenship is allowed in the U.S., as ruled in ***Afroyim v. Rusk***.[41]

Various countries around the world have their citizenships for sale, either for direct purchase or for a termed "investment." Samples of these values are:[42]

---

[41]387 U.S. 253 (1967)
[42]http://www.isla-offshore.com/second-passport/eu-citizenship-facts/

Dominica—$100,000[43]

Bulgaria—$125,000[44]

Albania—$200,000[45]

St. Kitts and Nevis—$250,000[46,47]

Hungary—$325,000[48]

Cyprus—$430,000[49]

Montenegro—$650,000[50]

The fact that these countries have many purchasers tells us there is significant economic value to multiple citizenships.

---

[43] http://newcitizenship.org/english/FAQs/tabid/78/language/en-US/Default.aspx

[44] http://www.huffingtonpost.com/huff-wires/20121130/eu-bulgaria-citizenship-for-sale/

[45] http://www.themovechannel.com/news/stories/242002c000-citizenship-offer-to-boost-albania-in-2013/#.UeRKW9LVB8E

[46] http://www.digitaljournal.com/article/343427

[47] http://www.royalgazette.com/article/20130228/BUSINESS/702289963

[48] http://www.reuters.com/article/2012/10/30/hungary-bonds-citizenship-idUSL5E8LU33Q20121030

[49] http://www.balkans.com/open-news.php?uniquenumber=170078

[50] http://www.businessweek.com/ap/financialnews/D9HGPRA81.htm

BENEFITS OF DUAL CITIZENSHIP

Benefits need to be determined by the individual applicant. Some that bear consideration are:

1. Retention of a heritage right
2. Security and safety—see Mumbai bombings, Leon Klinghoffer, Boston Bombers
3. Protections by more than one government (see Gilad Shalit)
4. Resident rates at universities within the EU
5. Visa-free travel / reduced entry and exit fees
6. Faster lines in immigration
7. Right to live and work anywhere in the European Union
8. Ability to change citizenships within the EU
9. Options for where you want to live
10. Health insurance
11. Reduction in bureaucracy
12. Right to pass on citizenship to the next generation
13. Connection to heritage and keeping memory alive
14. Right to own property
15. Access to retirement programs
16. Property restitution claims
17. Tax benefits
18. Right to participate in political life[51]

---

[51] http://www.presseurop.eu/en/content/article/1382341-multiple-citizenship-way-future

NEGATIVES OF DUAL CITIZENSHIP

Negatives need to be determined by the individual applicant. Some that bear consideration are:

1. Impedes right of U.S. to intervene if citizen is in that country
2. Possible tax issues
3. Security clearances
4. Conscription
5. Child custody laws may be different in case of divorce
6. Person may receive benefits to which they are not entitled

PART II

DUAL CITIZENSHIP IN EUROPE

This document is intended for general informational purposes only, and nothing contained in this document is intended to offer or to provide legal advice or counsel. If you desire or seek legal advice or counsel, you should consult with appropriate legal counsel regarding your individual situation. All information provided is deemed reliable but is not guaranteed and should be independently verified. Sources of data are from the Internet, Embassies, and Consulates worldwide.

Data current as of June 1, 2013.

AUSTRIA

Austria is a Federal Republic in East Central Europe. It is bordered by the Czech Republic, Germany, Hungary, Slovakia, Slovenia, Italy, Switzerland, and Liechtenstein. Austria covers 83,855 square kilometers (32,377 sq. mi) with a population of approximately 8.5 million people. Austria had a pre WWII Jewish population of approximately 185,000, of which approximately 50,000 were murdered during the Holocaust.

- Jus sanguinis – Either parent is a citizen
- Were forced to leave Austria before May 9, 1945 (suffered from or feared Nazi persecution)
- Dual citizenship permitted in limited cases (ex. if born to Austrian parents in foreign country)

Persons who had to fear or suffered persecution by the NSDAP and/or the authorities of the Third Reich or who had to fear or suffered persecution because of defending the democratic Republic of Austria and left Austria before May 9th, 1945 may reacquire their Austrian citizenship based on Section 58c of the Austrian Nationality Act. Neither permanent residence in Austria nor renouncing present citizenship are required; no fee will be charged.

Regaining citizenship by Declaration based on Sec. 58c has to be done in writing by a standardized notification form together with several supporting documents. Competent authorities: Vienna: Mat der Wiener Landesregierung, Magistratsabteilung 35 or the competent Austrian Embassy/Consulate General.

Please note: Some victims do not apply for themselves, but for their children (or their children apply personally). These cases then do no longer fall in the category Victims of Nazi persecution (Regaining citizenship by Declaration based on Sec. 58c) since for that matter a determination procedure ("Feststellungsverfahren") has to be done.

A child born to Austrian parents is an Austrian citizen. If the parents are married at the time of birth, Austrian citizenship of either the mother or the father is sufficient, so long as the child was born after January 9, 1983. For children born prior to that date, the father must have been an Austrian citizen: children born to an Austrian mother married to a non-Austrian father do not qualify. If the parents are not married, however, a father cannot pass on Austrian citizenship, whereas a mother can. Should the parents happen to marry at some time after the birth, citizenship is automatically granted to the child retroactively. If the child is over 14 at that time, however, the child's consent is needed.

Citizenship of the European Union
Austrian citizens are also citizens of the European Union and thus enjoy rights of free movement and have the right to vote in elections for the European Parliament.

BELGIUM

Belgium is a federal state in Western Europe. It is a founding member of the European Union and hosts the EU's headquarters as well as those of several other major international organizations such as NATO. Belgium covers an area of 30,528 square kilometers (11,787 sq. mi), and it has a population of about 11 million people. The Brussels-Capital Region, officially bilingual, is a mostly French-speaking enclave within the Flemish Region. A German-speaking Community exists in eastern Wallonia. Belgium's linguistic diversity and related political conflicts are reflected in the political history and a complex system of government.

Belgium had a pre WWII Jewish population of approximately 66,000, of which approximately 28,900 were murdered during the Holocaust.

- Jus sanguinis and Jus soli typically required - Either parent is a citizen and born in Belgium
- Dual citizenship allowed for those gaining foreign nationality after April 28, 2008. Certain restrictions apply prior to that date.

Belgian citizenship is based on a mixture of the principles of Jus sanguinis and Jus soli. In other words, both place of birth and Belgian parentage are relevant for determining whether a person is a Belgian citizen. It is regulated by the Code of Belgian Nationality.

In some circumstances citizenship is granted to children born in Belgium to non-Belgian parents. This is not the case where parents are temporary or short term visitors

Birth in Belgium

A person born in Belgium (to non-Belgian parents) is a Belgian citizen if that person:

- holds no other nationality at the time of birth (i.e., is stateless) OR;

- loses any other nationality before turning 18 OR;

- has a parent who was born in Belgium or who has lived in Belgium for at least five years during the last 10 years OR;

- is adopted (while under 18) by a parent holding another nationality who was born in Belgium and who has had their main place of residence in Belgium for five years during the 10 year period before the adoption takes effect.

- has two parents or adoptive parents born abroad who submitted a declaration before that person's twelfth birthday requesting that the person be granted Belgian nationality. Belgium must have been the parents' main place of residence during the 10 years preceding the declaration, and the person must have lived in Belgium since birth.

Effectively this means that:

- the children of long-resident immigrants can acquire Belgian citizenship

- the grandchildren of immigrants to Belgium are normally Belgian by birth

Birth to a Belgian parent

Access to Belgian citizenship depends on one's date of birth:

Before 1 January 1967

Belgian citizenship is acquired by:

- the legitimate child of a father who is a Belgian citizen OR;

- a person born outside wedlock who was acknowledged by one's mother who is a Belgian citizen, at least until being acknowledged by one's father (if happening before majority age : 21 years old). That person is definitely Belgian after one's majority if no change occurred.

1 January 1967 to 31 December 1984

Belgian citizenship is acquired by:

- birth in Belgium to a Belgian citizen OR;

- birth outside Belgium where the person is the legitimate child of a father who is a Belgian citizen OR;

- birth outside Belgium to a mother who is a Belgian citizen and who was born in Belgium or in Belgian Congo before 30 June 1960 or in Rwanda or Burundi before 1 July 1962.

On or after 1 January 1985

Belgian citizenship is acquired by:

birth in Belgium to a Belgian citizen OR;

One was born abroad AND:

1. the Belgian parent was born in Belgium or in Belgian Congo before 30 June 1960 or in Rwanda or Burundi before 1 July 1962 OR;

2. the Belgian parent was born abroad and makes a declaration, within a period of five years following the child's birth, requesting that he be granted Belgian nationality. This declaration must be submitted to the Belgian embassy or consulate in the main place of residence of the Belgian parent abroad, or the registrar in the parent's municipality (if the parent lives in Belgium). Belgian nationality is obtained on the date upon which the declaration is made.

Where a person is born outside Belgium and the Belgian parent who was born abroad does not submit a "déclaration d'attribution/toekenningsverklaring" within a period of five years following the child's birth, a late declaration is allowed provided the child does not have another. If the child acquires another nationality before age 18, Belgian nationality is lost.

Naturalization as a Belgian citizen

Belgium's nationality changed in late 2012. The information below is obsolete.

A person may be naturalized as a Belgian citizen after three years residence in Belgium.

- This period is reduced to two years for political refugees and stateless persons.

- Residence abroad can be equated with residence in Belgium if one can prove that one had genuine ties with Belgium during the periods stipulated above.

Normally a person must be aged 18 or over in order to become a naturalized Belgian citizen. Unemancipated minors obtain Belgian citizenship automatically at the same time a responsible parent is naturalized.

Where a person is married to a Belgian citizen for over three years, and has held a permit allowing settlement in Belgium for that period, the residence period for naturalization may be reduced to 6 months.

Belgian citizenship by declaration

This is a simplified form of naturalization for certain people with special ties to Belgium.

Nationality declaration

From the age of 18 a person can obtain Belgian nationality by signing a nationality declaration if that person meets one of the following criteria:

- born in Belgium and with main place of residence in Belgium, without any interruptions, birth OR;

- one was born abroad to a Belgian citizen parent OR;

- the person has had a main place of residence in Belgium for at least seven years and has an unlimited residence permit or authorization to settle in Belgium.

The nationality declaration can only be signed in front of the registrar in the applicant's municipality in Belgium. This declaration cannot be approved by a Belgian embassy or consulate.

Opting for Belgian nationality between 18 and 22 years of age

A person aged between 18 and 22 can sign a declaration indicating opting for Belgian nationality if that person meets one of the following criteria:

- born in Belgium OR;

- born abroad and one of the person's adoptive parents is a Belgian citizen at the time the declaration opting for Belgian nationality is made OR;

- born abroad and one of the person's parents or adoptive parents was a Belgian citizen when the person was born OR;

- born abroad and with a main place of residence in Belgium with the person's parents or adoptive parents for at least one year before the child turned six.

All applicants must also meet the following criteria:

- main place of residence must have been in Belgium during the 12 month period preceding the declaration; and

- main place of residence in Belgium either between the ages of 14 and 18 or for a period of at least nine years. The applicant is exempt from these latter two criteria if one the person's parents or adoptive parents was a Belgian citizen or had previously held Belgian citizenship at the time of the person's birth.

Residence abroad can be equated with residence in Belgium if one can prove that one has genuine ties with Belgium.

Belgian citizenship by marriage

Since 1 January 1985, marriage does not give any direct claim to Belgian citizenship. However, he or she may request Belgian nationality after the marriage has taken place.[52]

Belgian citizenship by adoption

From 1 January 1988, children adopted by Belgian citizens generally acquire Belgian citizenship on the same basis as those born to Belgian citizens. Different rules apply for adoptions completed prior to 1988.

Loss of Belgian citizenship

---

[52]Belgian nationality: 06. Am I a Belgian citizen through marriage?", General Info: Citizenship, Embassy of Belgium in London

A person at least 18 years old who voluntarily obtained another nationality before 9 June 2007 automatically lost their Belgian nationality. A person at least 18 years old who voluntarily obtained the nationality of Austria, Denmark, France, Ireland, Italy, Luxembourg, the Netherlands, Norway, Spain or the United Kingdom between 9 June 2007 and 28 April 2008 automatically lost their Belgian nationality. A person who voluntarily obtains another nationality after 28 April 2008 will no longer lose their Belgian nationality, regardless of the nationality acquired. It is also possible to lose Belgian citizenship in the following circumstances.

Dual citizenship

Since 28 April 2008, Belgian law permits all Belgian nationals to obtain any other nationality without losing their Belgian nationality (unless the law about the other newly acquired citizenship or nationality requires the loss, of course).

Citizenship of the European Union

Belgian citizens are also citizens of the European Union and thus enjoy rights of free movement and have the right to vote in elections for the European Parliament.

BULGARIA

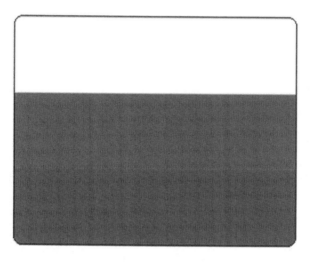

Bulgaria is a country located in Southeastern Europe. It is bordered by Romania to the north, Serbia and Macedonia to the west, Greece and Turkey to the south and the Black Sea to the east. With a territory of 110,994 square kilometers (42,855 sq. mi), Bulgaria is Europe's 14th-largest country. Its location has made it a historical crossroad for various civilizations and as such it is the home of some of the earliest metalworking, religious and other cultural artifacts in the world.[53] Bulgaria had a pre WWII Jewish population of approximately 50,000, who were protected and saved by the Bulgarian king, government, and people.

---

[53]"Development of metallurgy in Eurasia." Department of Prehistory and Europe, British Museum. p. 1015. Retrieved 8 June 2012. "In contrast, the earliest exploitation and working of gold occurs in the Balkans during the mid-fifth millennium BC, several centuries after the earliest known copper smelting. This is demonstrated most spectacularly in the various objects adorning the burials at Varna, Bulgaria (Renfrew 1986; Highamet al. 2007). In contrast, the earliest gold objects found in Southwest Asia date only to the beginning of the fourth millennium BC as at Nahal Qanah in Israel (Golden 2009), suggesting that gold exploitation may have been a Southeast European invention, albeit a short-lived one.

- Jus sanguinis - Either parent is a citizen
- Limited jus soli – Born in Bulgaria
- Dual citizenship allowed

Article 25 of the 1991 constitution specifies that a "person of Bulgarian origin shall acquire Bulgarian citizenship through a facilitated procedure." Article 15 of the Law on Bulgarian Citizenship provides that an individual "of Bulgarian origin" (ethnicity) may be naturalized without any waiting period and without having to show a source of income, knowledge of the Bulgarian language, or renunciation of his former citizenship. This approach has been a tradition since the foundation of Bulgaria in 1879, when large numbers of ethnic Bulgarians remained outside of the state. Bulgaria and Greece were subject to a population exchange following the Second Balkan War. The conditions of the treaty settlement mandated that they accept individuals claiming respective ethnic origin.

CZECH REPUBLIC

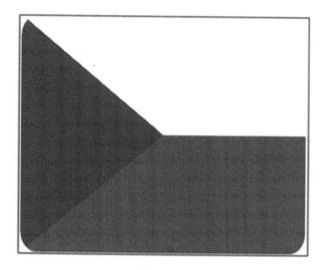

The Czech Republic is a landlocked country in Central Europe. The country is bordered by Germany to the west, Austria to the south, Slovakia to the east and Poland to the north. Its capital and largest city, with 1.3 million inhabitants, is Prague. The Czech Republic includes the historical territories of Bohemia and Moravia and a small part of Silesia. The Czech Republic (then Bohemia and Moravia) had a pre WWII Jewish population of approximately 118,310, of which approximately 78,150 were murdered during the Holocaust.

- Jus sanguinis - Either parent is a citizen
- Dual citizenship limited

Citizenship by birth

The principle of Jus sanguinis is used to determine eligibility for citizenship, as is typical in Europe. In principle, any person born to a Czech citizen is a Czech citizen at birth. Whether the person is born in the Czech Republic or elsewhere is irrelevant. Where only the father is Czech, and the parents are unmarried, proof of paternity is required - by the parents making a concerted declaration before the Registry Office or a court. Children born in the Czech Republic to non-Czech parents do not acquire Czech citizenship unless: the parents are stateless; and at least one parent is a permanent resident of the Czech Republic

Children aged less than 15 years found on the territory of the Czech Republic (where identity of the parents cannot be established) are deemed to be Czech citizens.

Emigrants

During the communist era (1948–89) hundreds of thousands of Czechoslovakian citizens had emigrated into the West. The regime punished emigration by removing Czechoslovak citizenship, along with property confiscation and in absentia prison sentences. Since the Velvet Revolution in 1989, many emigrants demanded their citizenship be restored. Between 1999 and 2004, a special measure allowed them to regain the citizenship, but a few people took advantage of the wording, which "granted" citizenship rather than "restored" it and so got dual citizenship. A few people from Volhynia and Romania also got citizenship.

Declaration

If a person was a citizen of the Czech and Slovak Federal Republic as of 31 December 1992, he may declare citizenship of either the Czech Republic or Slovakia (gaining Slovak citizenship) assuming he does not have any other citizenship. The Slovak provision allowing for this grant expired in 1993, however the Czech equivalent remains in the citizenship law.

Note: Census of Population and Housing 2011: Basic final results. Czech Statistical Office. Retrieved on 19 December, 2012.

DENMARK

Denmark is a state in the Scandinavian region of Northern Europe with the two autonomous constituent countries in the north Atlantic Ocean, the Faroe Islands and Greenland. Denmark is the southernmost of the Nordic countries, located southwest of Sweden, south of Norway and bordered to the south by Germany. Denmark consists of a peninsula, Jutland, and the Danish archipelago of 407 islands, which includes Zealand, Vendsyssel-Thy, Funen, Lolland, Falster and Bornholm. The national language, Danish, is closely related to Swedish and Norwegian.[54] Denmark had a pre WWII Jewish population of approximately 7,800, of which approximately 60 were murdered during the Holocaust.

- Jus sanguinis - Either parent is a citizen and born in Denmark.

- Dual citizenship limited, current government reviewing lifting restrictions

---

[54]"Denmark in numbers 2010." Statistics Denmark. Retrieved 2 May 2013.

Danish nationality law is ruled by the Constitutional act of Denmark (of 1953) and the Consolidated Act of Danish Nationality (of 2003, with amendment in 2004).

Danish nationality can be acquired in one of the following ways:

Automatically at birth if born in Denmark and at least one of the parents has Danish citizenship.

Automatically at birth if born outside Denmark and the mother has Danish citizenship.

Automatically at birth if born outside Denmark and the father has Danish citizenship and is married to the mother.

Automatically if a person is adopted as a child under 12 years of age

By declaration for nationals of another Nordic country

By naturalization, that is, by statute

Danish nationality can be lost in one of the following ways:

Automatically if a person voluntarily acquires nationality of another country (whether after application or by entering the public service of another country)

Automatically for an unmarried child under the age of 18 years upon acquisition of a foreign nationality in the setting of a parent who has acquired a foreign nationality and thereby lost his or her Danish nationality

Automatically if a person acquired Danish nationality by birth, but was not born in Denmark and has never lived in Denmark by the age of 22 years (unless this would render the person stateless or the person has lived in another Nordic country for an aggregate period of no less than 7 years)

By court order if a person acquired his or her Danish nationality by fraudulent conduct

By court order if a person is convicted of violation of one or more provisions of Parts 12 and 13 of the Danish Criminal Code (crimes against national security), unless this would render the person stateless

By voluntary application to the Minister for Refugee, Immigration and Integration Affairs (a person who is or who desires to become a national of a foreign country may be released from his or her Danish nationality by such an application)

Naturalization as a Danish citizen

One must have permanent residence status in Denmark in order to become a citizen, except in a few circumstances (e.g. adopted children). For non-EU citizens, the qualifying rules for permanent residence are quite restrictive, requiring a full-time physical employment for at least 2.5 years despite having adequate income from other sources.

9 years of continuous residence, with restricted allowance for interrupted residence of up to 1 year or 2 years in special circumstances (education, family illness). Continuous residence is not clearly defined, but apparently one must state periods of absence from Denmark longer than 14 days.

8 years of continuous residence for people who are stateless or with refugee status

Each year of marriage to a Danish citizen reduces the requirement by one year, to a maximum reduction of 3 years. For example, as little as 6 years of continuous uninterrupted residence for people who are married to Danish nationals for 3 years. One year of cohabitation before marriage counts as a year of marriage for this purpose.

There is a special and little mentioned clause which allows for absences from Denmark of longer than 1 or 2 years if one is married to a Danish citizen. The total period of continuous residence should be at least 3 years and it must exceed the total periods of absence, AND either: the period of marriage being at least 2 years or the total period of residence in Denmark being 10 years less the period of marriage and 1 year for cohabitation before marriage). One must still have permanent residence.

If one is married to a Dane who must work in a foreign country 'for Danish interests', then the period of absence from Denmark can be regarded as residence in Denmark.

Multiple citizenship

Currently, it is a fundamental principle in the legislation to restrict dual nationality as much as possible.[55] One exception to this is if a person is born of a Danish parent in a country that grants citizenship under the principle of jus soli. In October 2011, the newly elected center-left coalition government has indicated its intention to permit dual citizenship.

Citizenship of the European Union

Danish citizens are also citizens of the European Union and thus enjoy rights of free movement and have the right to vote in elections for the European Parliament.

---

[55]"Dual nationality (in Denmark)". Retrieved 8 July 2012.

ESTONIA

Estonia is a state in the Baltic region of Northern Europe. It is bordered to the north by the Gulf of Finland, to the west by the Baltic Sea, to the south by Latvia (343 km), and to the east by Lake Peipus and Russia (338.6 km).[56] Estonia had a pre WWII Jewish population of approximately 4,500, of which approximately 1,750 were murdered during the Holocaust. Estonia was the first country to be declared Judenrein by the Nazis.

- Jus sanguinis – Descent without limits
- Dual citizenship limited

Estonian citizenship - based primarily on the principle of jus sanguinis - is governed by the 19th January 1995 law promulgated by the Riigikogu which took effect on the 1st April 1995. The Citizenship and Migration Board (Estonia) is responsible for processing applications and enquiries concerning Estonian citizenship.

Resolution Concerning the Citizenship of the Democratic Republic of

---

[56]Estonian Republic. Official website of the Republic of Estonia (in Estonian)

Estonia, the first Estonian citizenship law was adopted by the Estonian National Council on November 26, 1918. According to the law all people who

1) were permanent residents on the day the law came into force on the territory of the Republic of Estonia;

2) prior to the Estonian Declaration of Independence on 24 February 1918 had been subjects of the Russian State;

3) were entered in the parish registers or originated from the territory of Estonia, regardless of their ethnicity and faith were proclaimed Estonian citizens.

Eligibility for Estonian citizenship

> ➤ By descent - Children born to parents, at least one of whom was Estonian citizen at the time of birth (regardless of the place of birth) are automatically considered Estonian citizens by descent.

> ➤ By place of birth - Children born in Estonia to stateless or unknown parents at the time of birth are eligible for Estonian citizenship with no conflicts at all.

> ➤ By marriage - A woman who married an Estonian citizen before the 26th February 1992 is eligible for Estonian citizenship.

> ➤ By naturalization - Those seeking to become Estonian citizens via naturalization require to fulfill the following criteria:

> ➤ applicant is aged 15 or over

> ➤ resided in Estonia legally for at least eight years and from that last five years permanent stay in Estonia

> ➤ be familiar in the Estonian language. People who have graduated from an Estonian-speaking high school or an institute of higher education are assumed to fulfill this criterion without the need to take a full examination.

> ➤ take an examination demonstrating familiarity with the Estonian Constitution

➤ showing a demonstrated means of support
➤ taking an oath of loyalty

Those who have committed serious crimes or are foreign military personnel on active duty are ineligible to seek naturalization as an Estonian citizen.

Duties and rights of Estonian citizenship

Male Estonian citizens are required to take up national service

Undefined citizenship

'Undefined citizenship' is a term used in Estonia to denote a post-Soviet form of statelessness. It is applied to those migrants from former Soviet republics and their children, who were unable or unwilling to pursue any country's citizenship after the collapse of the Soviet Union. Russia being a successor state to the Soviet Union, all former USSR citizens qualified for citizenship of Russian Federation, available upon mere request, as provided by the law "On the RSFSR Citizenship" in force up to end of 2000.Estonia's policy of requiring naturalization of post-war immigrants was in part influenced by Russia's citizenship law and the desire to prevent dual citizenship.[57]

Stateless persons who reside legally in Estonia can apply for an alien's passport. Estonian alien's passport allows visa-free travel within Schengen treaty countries for a maximum of 90 days in a 6 month period.

Dual nationality

Although not legally permitted, some naturalized Estonian citizens also possess another, e.g., Russian citizenship. According to law, acquiring a foreign citizenship voluntarily and entering into a military or civilian service for another state constitute forfeiture of Estonian

---

[57]Wayne C. Thompson, Citizenship and borders: Legacies of Soviet empire in Estonia, Journal of Baltic Studies, Volume 29, Issue 2 Summer 1998 , pages 109 - 134

citizenship. In effect, this forfeiture requirement applies to naturalized Estonian citizens only, because, according to the constitution, Estonian citizenship obtained by descent is inalienable and cannot be taken away by anyone else other than the citizenship holder.

Citizenship of the European Union

Estonian citizens are also citizens of the European Union and thus enjoy rights of free movement and have the right to vote in elections for the European Parliament.

FINLAND

Finland is a Nordic country situated in the Fennoscandian region of Northern Europe. It is bordered by Sweden to the west, Norway to the north and Russia to the east, while Estonia lies to the south across the Gulf of Finland. Finland had a pre WWII Jewish population of approximately 2,000, of which 7 were murdered during the Holocaust.

- Jus sanguinis - Either parent is a citizen
- Dual citizenship permitted since June 1, 2003

Jews issued full equal rights in Finland in 1917.

During WWII: Germany's Ambassador to Helsinki concluded in a report that Finns would not endanger their citizens of Jewish origin in any situation. Yad Vashem records that 22 Finnish Jews died in the Holocaust, although all of them died fighting for the Finnish Army.

Citizenship of Finland can be obtained on the basis of birth, marriage of parents, adoption, or the place of birth. In addition, it may be acquired by application or by declaration to authorities. Finnish citizenship acquisition is based primarily on the legal principle of jus sanguinis. However, for many practical purposes, the concepts of municipal domicile and domicile in Finland are as important to the relation between the individual and the Finnish authorities as the individual's citizenship status.

Finnish law provides a right of return to ethnic Finns from the former Soviet Union, including Ingrians. Applicants must now pass an examination in one of the official languages of the country, Finnish or Swedish. Certain persons of Finnish descent who live outside the former Soviet Union also have the right to establish permanent residency, which would eventually entitle them to qualify for citizenship.

FRANCE

France is a unitary semi-presidential republic located mostly in Western Europe, with several overseas regions and territories. Metropolitan France extends from the Mediterranean Sea to the English Channel and the North Sea, and from the Rhine to the Atlantic Ocean. From its shape, it is often referred to in French as l'Hexagone ("The Hexagon"). France had a pre WWII Jewish population of approximately 350,000, of which approximately 77,320 were murdered during the Holocaust.

- Jus sanguinis - Either parent is a citizen
- Jus soli with certain restrictions in place
- Dual citizenship permitted

French nationality law is historically based on the principles of jus soli (Latin for "right of soil"), according to Ernest Renan's definition, in opposition to the German definition of nationality, Jus sanguinis (Latin for "right of blood"), formalized by Fichte.

The 1993 Méhaignerie Law required children born in France of foreign parents to request French nationality at adulthood, rather than being automatically accorded citizenship. This "manifestation of will" requirement was subsequently abrogated by the Guigou Law of 1998, but children born in France of foreign parents remain foreign until obtaining legal majority.

Children born in France to tourists or short-term visitors do not acquire French citizenship by virtue of birth in France: residency must be proven. As immigration became increasingly a political theme in the 1980s, albeit accompanied by a lower immigration rate (see Demographics in France), both left-wing and right-wing governments have issued several laws restricting the possibilities of being naturalized.

Attribution of French nationality

The attribution of French nationality due to filiation. (Jus sanguinis)

The attribution of French nationality by birth in France (Jus soli) if other requirements (such as residence in France) are also met.

Filiation

Plenary adoption is the only act of filiation which carries direct effects on nationality. Unlike the process of simple adoption, a child adopted according to the procedure of plenary adoption breaks any bond with his family of origin.[58]

Filiation must be established while the child is a minor to take effect. Consequently, the recognition of a child older than the age of majority has no effect on his or her nationality.

Birth in France

Children born in France (including overseas territories) to at least one

---

[58]Civil Code of France, Article 343

parent who is also born in France automatically acquire French citizenship at birth (double jus soli).

A child born in France to foreign parents may acquire French citizenship:

at birth, if stateless.

at 18, if resident in France with at least 5 years' residence since age 11.

at 16 upon request by the child and if resident in France.

at 13 upon request by the child's parents and if resident in France.

if born in France of parents born before independence in a colony/territory in the past under French sovereignty.

at birth, if born in France before January 1, 1994.

at age 18, if born in France on or after January 1, 1994.

A child who was born abroad and who has only one French parent can repudiate his French nationality during the six months prior to his or her reaching the age of majority, or in the year which follows it (article 19-4 of the Civil Code).

Acquisition of French nationality

Naturalization

A person aged 18 or above may apply for French citizenship by naturalization after five years' habitual and continuous residence in France (if married and with children, then the applicant must be living in France with his/her family). In addition, it is required that the applicant has his/her primary source of income in France during the five-year period. Those applying who are not European Union, European Economic Area or Swiss nationals are required to be in possession of a "titre de séjour" (a residence permit).

The residence period may be completely waived for those who have served in the French military, for refugees, or in other exceptional cases.[59]

The residence period can be reduced to two years for a person who has completed two years of post-graduate education in France or who has rendered exceptional service to France through their talents and abilities.

Naturalization will only be successful for those who are judged to have integrated into French society (i.e. by virtue of language skills and understanding of rights and responsibilities of a French citizen, to be demonstrated during an interview at the local prefecture), and who show loyalty to French institutions.

Naturalization through residency is accorded by publication of a decree in the Journal Officiel by decision of the Home Ministry and the prefecture of the region where the applicant has submitted his/her application. There is an obligatory delay of 18 months from the date of submission before the applicant is notified of the result of his/her naturalization application.

Attribution of French nationality

Through parentage (right of blood) , Through birth in France (law of place of birth) , Through marriage

French Citizenship and identity

This section does not cite any references or sources. Please help improve this section by adding citations to reliable sources. Unsourced material may be challenged and removed. (September 2009) According to the French Republic, the French people are those who are in possession of French nationality. According to the French Constitution, "France shall be an indivisible, secular, democratic and social Republic. It shall ensure the equality of all citizens before the law, without

---

[59]Naturalization : conditions à remplir - Service-public.fr

distinction of origin, race or religion. It shall respect all beliefs. It shall be organized on a decentralized basis." Article 1

Since the middle of the 19th century, France has exhibited a very high rate of immigration, mainly from Southern Europe, Eastern Europe, the Maghreb, Africa and Asia. According to a 2004 report by INED researcher Michèle Tribalat France has approximately 14 million persons (out of nearly 63 million) (see demographics of France) of foreign ascendancy (immigrants or with at least one parent or great-parent immigrant), mostly black or Muslim.

The absence of official statistics on French citizens of foreign origin is not coincidental. Under French law passed after the Vichy regime, it is forbidden to categorize people according to their ethnic origins. In France, as in many European countries, censuses do not collect information on supposed ancestry. Moreover, all French statistics are forbidden to have any references concerning ethnic membership. Thus, the French government's assimilationist stance towards immigration as well as towards regional identities and cultures, together with the political heritage of the French revolution has led to the development of a French identity which is based more on the notion of citizenship than on cultural, historical or ethnic ties.

For this reason, French identity must not necessarily be associated with the "ethnic French people", but can be associated with either a nationality and citizenship, or a culture and language-based group. The latter forms the basis for La Francophone, a group of French-speaking countries, or countries with historical and cultural association to France. The concept of "French ethnicity" exists outside France's borders, in particular in Quebec where some people claim membership to a "French ethnic group", but here again many view it as not so much ethnicity-based as language-based, and would also include immigrants from, for example, Haiti. France's particular self-perception means that French identity may include a naturalized, French-speaking ethnic Portuguese or Algerian. Nonetheless, like in other European countries, some level of discrimination does occur, and there are higher unemployment rates among job-seekers with foreign-sounding names.

Rights and obligations of French citizens

In modern France in general the rights are fundamentally the same as those in other EU countries.

Despite this official discourse of universality, French nationality has not meant automatic citizenship. Some categories of French people have been excluded, throughout the years, from full citizenship:

Women: until the Liberation, they were deprived of the right to vote. The provisional government of General de Gaulle accorded them this right by the April 21, 1944 prescription. A law passed on June 6, 2000 attempted to address the economic disparity between men and women.

Military: for a long time, it was named the Grande muette ("The Big Mute") in reference to its prohibition from interfering in political life. During a large part of the Third Republic (1871–1940), the Army was in its majority anti-republican (and thus counterrevolutionary). The Dreyfus Affair and the May 16, 1877 crisis that led to a monarchist coup d'état by MacMahon, are examples of this anti-republican spirit. Therefore, they would gain the right to vote only with the August 17, 1945 prescription: the contribution of De Gaulle to the interior French Resistance reconciled the Army with the Republic. Nevertheless, militaries do not benefit from the whole of public liberties, as the July 13, 1972 law on the general statute of militaries specify.

Young people: the July 1974 law instituted at the instigation of president Valéry Giscard d'Estaing reduced to 18 years the coming of age, which thus made of these teenagers full citizens.

Naturalized foreigners. Since January 9, 1973, foreigners who have acquired French nationality do not have to wait five years after their naturalization to be able to vote.

Inhabitants of the colonies. The May 7, 1946 law meant that soldiers from the "Empire" (such as the tirailleurs) killed during World War I and World War II were not citizens.

Furthermore, some authors who have insisted on the "crisis of the nation-state" allege that nationality and citizenship are becoming separate concepts. They show as example "international", "supranational citizenship" or "world citizenship" (membership to transnational organizations, such as Amnesty International or Greenpeace NGOs). This would indicate a path toward a "postnational citizenship".[60]

Beside this, modern citizenship is linked to civic participation (also called positive freedom), which design voting, demonstrations, petitions, activism, etc. Therefore, social exclusion may lead to deprive one of his/her citizenship. This has led various authors (Philippe Van Parijs, Jean-Marc Ferry, Alain Caillé, André Gorz) to theorize a guaranteed minimum income which would impede exclusion from citizenship.

Dual citizenship

Dual citizenship has been permitted since 1973. Possession of one or more other nationalities, does not, in principle, affect the French nationality. France denounced the Chapter I of the Council of Europe Convention on the Reduction of Cases of Multiple Nationality and on Military Obligations in Cases of Multiple Nationality of May 6, 1963. The denunciation took effect March 5, 2009.

Citizenship of the European Union

French citizens are also citizens of the European Union and thus enjoy rights of free movement and have the right to vote in elections for the European Parliament.

---

[60](French) B. Villalba. "Chapitre 2 - Les incertitudes de la citoyenneté." Catholic University of Lille, Law Department. Retrieved 2006-05-03.

GERMANY

Germany is a federal parliamentary republic in western-central Europe. The country consists of 16 states, and its capital and largest city is Berlin. Germany covers an area of 357,021 square kilometers (137,847 sq. mi) and has a largely temperate seasonal climate. With 81.8 million inhabitants, it is the most populous member state in the European Union. Germany had a pre WWII Jewish population of approximately 566,000, of which approximately 134,500 – 141,500 were murdered during the Holocaust.

- *Jus sanguinis - Either parent is a citizen*
- *Persons that lost citizenship under Nazi persecution can regain German citizenship.*
- *Also available for their decedents*
- *Dual citizenship permitted in certain circumstances*

German citizenship is based primarily on the principle of jus sanguinis.

In other words one usually acquires German citizenship if a parent is a German citizen, irrespective of place of birth.

Birth in Germany

Children born on or after 1 January 2000 to non-German parents acquire German citizenship at birth if at least one parent: has a permanent residence permit; and has been residing in Germany for at least eight years.

Such children will be required to apply successfully to retain German citizenship by the age of 23. Assuming this law is not changed or overturned by a court, these persons will normally be required to prove they do not hold any other foreign citizenship. The only exceptions are EU citizens and citizens of countries where it is impossible to lose your citizenship, like Morocco or Iran, for example.

Parents who are citizens of European Economic Area states or Switzerland are eligible to receive permanent resident permits after five years.

Descent from a German parent

A person born of a parent with German citizenship at the time of the child's birth is a German citizen. Place of birth is not a factor in citizenship determination based on parentage.

Adoption

A child adopted by a German citizen becomes German national automatically if aged less than 18 on the date the application for adoption was made. So dual citizenship is granted.

Naturalization as a German citizen

Naturalization by entitlement

An individual who fulfills all of the following criteria has an entitlement to naturalize as a German citizen:[61]

he/she has been ordinarily resident in Germany for at least 8 years (this period can be reduced - see below)

he/she has legal capacity or a legal representative

confirms his/her present and past commitment to the free democratic constitutional system enshrined in the German Basic Law (or that he is presently committed to such principles and has departed from former support of ideas contrary to such principles)

he/she is a European Union or Swiss citizen in possession of the appropriate residence permit which permits the free movement of persons, or he/she is a non-EU/Swiss citizen who has been granted a permanent right of residence

he/she is able to support himself/herself without recourse to benefits

he/she has not been sentenced for an unlawful act and is not subject to any court order imposing a measure of reform and prevention

he/she possesses an adequate knowledge of German

possesses knowledge of the legal system, the society and living conditions in the Federal Republic of Germany

An individual who does not have legal capacity is entitled to naturalize as a German citizen merely through ordinary residence in Germany for at least 8 years - he/she does not have to fulfill the other criteria (e.g. adequate command of the German language and ability to be self-supporting without recourse to benefits).

Applicants for naturalization are normally expected to prove they have renounced their existing nationality, or will lose this automatically upon

---

[61]http://www.bmi.bund.de/SharedDocs/Gesetzestexte/EN/Staatsangehoerigkeits gesetz_englisch.pdf?__blob=publicationFile

naturalization. An exception applies to those unable to give up their nationality easily (such as refugees). A further exception applies to citizens of Switzerland and the European Union member states.

An individual who is entitled to naturalize as a German citizen can also apply for his/her spouse and minor children to be naturalized at the same time (his/her spouse and minor children need not have ordinarily resided in Germany for at least 8 years).

Exceptions to the normal residence requirements include:

persons who have completed an integration course may have the residence requirement reduced to 7 years

If a person shows that he/she is especially well integrated and has a higher level of command of the German language than the basic requirement for the German citizenship (i.e., higher than B1) may have the residence requirement reduced to 6 years

The spouse of a German citizen may be naturalized after 3 years of continual residency in Germany. The marriage must have persisted for at least 2 years.

refugees and stateless persons may be able to apply after 6 years of continual residency

former German citizens

Naturalization by discretion

An individual who is ordinarily resident outside may be naturalized as a German citizen if he/she can demonstrate sufficient ties with Germany which justify his/her naturalization.[62]

Victims of Nazi persecution

Some people who lost German citizenship under the Nazi regime may

---

[62] "Germany Nationality Act, Section 14." Retrieved 2012-06-30.

be eligible for naturalization without requiring residence in Germany or renunciation of their existing citizenship. Children and grandchildren of such persons may also be eligible for German citizenship.

German-born children

Under transitional arrangements in the 1999 reforms (effective 1 January 2000), children who were born in Germany in 1990 or later, and would have been German had the law change been in force at the time, were entitled to be naturalized as German citizens.

An application for naturalization was required by 31 December 2000.

The child was required to apply for retention of German citizenship by age 23 and normally show that no other foreign citizenship was held at that time.

Loss of German citizenship

German citizenship is automatically lost when a German citizen voluntarily acquires the citizenship of another country. To this there are two exceptions:

When the German citizen acquires a nationality from within the European Union, Switzerland, or another country with which Germany has a corresponding treaty.

When permission to obtain a foreign citizenship has been applied for and granted in advance of foreign naturalization. A so-called permit to retain German citizenship must be obtained prior to naturalization. Failure to obtain a permit to retain German citizenship prior to naturalization results in the individual automatically losing German citizenship upon becoming a naturalized citizen of another country. [63]

---

[63] Information on obtaining/re-obtaining German citizenship for former German citizens and their descendants who were persecuted on political, racial or religious grounds between January 30, 1933 and May 8, 1945". German

Dual citizenship

Allowed under following circumstances:

If he/she is an EU or Swiss citizen during naturalization.

If he/she is a refugee and holds a 1951 travel document during naturalization.

where a child born to German parents acquires another citizenship at birth (e.g. based on place of birth, or descent from one parent)

where a naturalized German citizen, or a child born to non-German parents (non-EU or Swiss) in Germany, request and obtain a permission to keep his foreign nationality.

where a German citizen acquires a foreign nationality with the permission of the German government (e.g. existing relative ties or property in Germany or in the other country or if the occupation abroad requires domestic citizenship for execution)

Citizenship of the European Union

German citizens are also citizens of the European Union and thus enjoy rights of free movement and have the right to vote in elections for the European Parliament.

Consulates. Archived from the original on 19 August 2008. Retrieved 14 June 2011.

GREECE

Greece is a country in Southeast Europe. According to the 2011 census, Greece's population is around 11 million. Athens is the nation's capital and largest city, its urban area also including Piraeus. Greece had a pre WWII Jewish population of approximately 77,380, of which approximately 65,000 were murdered during the Holocaust.

- Jus sanguinis - Either parent is a citizen
- Dual citizenship allowed

Nationality law of Greece is based on the principle of jus sanguinis. Greek citizenship may be acquired by descent or through naturalization. Greek law permits dual citizenship. A Greek national is a citizen of the European Union, and therefore entitled to the same rights as other EU citizens.[64]

---

[64]"Southern Europe's Immigration Test." Time. Retrieved 2012-05-30.

Naturalization

A child of a Greek citizen acquires Greek nationality automatically at birth. The same applies to children born in Greece whose parents have lived legally and permanently in Greece for five years. Children born abroad and whose parents have lived legally and permanently in Greece for five years become Greek citizens upon successful completion of elementary education (six years). Greeks born abroad may transmit citizenship to their children from generation to generation indefinitely.

An alien born out of wedlock is automatically Greek if the mother is Greek (see matrilineality). If the father is Greek and paternity can be proven (for example, through a paternity test), the child will become Greek when an application is submitted for the child to become a Greek citizen, providing the child has not yet reached the age of 18. An alien who is over 18 may become Greek by naturalization.

A child over 18 of a Greek father does not require naturalization if they can establish a chain of Greek citizenship through properly recorded birth and marriage certificates.

An ethnic Greek born outside of Greece may acquire Greek citizenship by naturalization if they fail to qualify for simple registration as the child of a Greek citizen. (This provision excludes Greek Cypriots, who may seek Cypriot citizenship instead.) The applicant must prove that at least one parent or grandparent was born a Greek national.

Naturalization requirements are different for ethnic Greek and non-ethnic Greek aliens:

The alien ethnic Greek must make a declaration—in the presence of two witnesses, who must be Greek citizens—before the mayor or chairman of the village council where they live, which states they wish to be naturalized.

The alien may submit this declaration to the Greek consul of their domicile, who transmits it to the Ministry of the Interior with a relevant report.

An alien who is not an ethnic Greek must live in Greece for seven years before the declaration. They must also submit an application for naturalization to the Ministry of the Interior.

Children of a naturalized alien become Greeks if, at the time of completion of the naturalization proceedings, they are not married and are less than 18 year old.

A panel of Council of State (Supreme Court) judges has ruled that the citizenship law as described above, which allows foreigners who legally reside in Greece to vote and stand in local elections, is unconstitutional as only Greeks should be allowed this right.

Marriage

At present, marriage does not entail the acquisition or loss of Greek nationality. Before 1984, a woman marrying a Greek national became Greek automatically.

Naturalization by military service or monasticism in Mount Athos

Ethnic Greeks accepted to the military academies for officers or non-commissioned officers of the Greek armed forces (according to the special law governing each school) or who enlist in the armed forces as volunteers (according to the law governing each branch) acquire Greek nationality automatically from the time they enter the academies or are enlisted. Moreover, according to the Greek constitution, aliens admitted as monks in one of the monasteries of Mount Athos, become Greek automatically.

Loss of citizenship

A Greek national does not usually lose their Greek citizenship when they obtain another nationality, unless they request it. A Greek citizen may voluntarily renounce citizenship by submitting an application to the Ministry of Interior in Athens. For male Greek nationals, renunciation of citizenship is subject to the completion of their military duties.

Citizenship of the European Union

Greek citizens are also citizens of the European Union and thus enjoy rights of free movement and have the right to vote in elections for the European Parliament.

HUNGARY

Hungary is a landlocked country in Central Europe. It is situated in the Carpathian Basin and is bordered by Slovakia to the north, Ukraine, and Romania to the east, Serbia, and Croatia to the south, Slovenia to the southwest and Austria to the west. The country's capital, and largest city, is Budapest. Hungary is a member of the European Union, NATO, the OECD, the Visegrád Group, and the Schengen Agreement. The official language is Hungarian, also known as Magyar, which is part of the Finno-Ugric group and is the most widely spoken non-Indo-European language in Europe.[65] Hungary had a pre WWII Jewish population of approximately 825,000, of which approximately 560,000 were murdered during the Holocaust.

- Jus sanguinis – Ancestor was a citizen.

- Identify as Hungarian with proof

---

[65]Globally speaking: motives for adopting English vocabulary in other languages – Google Books. Google Books. Retrieved 20 September 2010.

- Dual citizenship permitted

Hungarian nationality law is based on the principles of jus sanguinis. Hungarian citizenship is acquired mainly on the basis of a Hungarian parent, or by naturalization. Children born in Hungary to foreign parents do not generally acquire Hungarian citizenship. Every Hungarian citizen is also a citizen of the European Union.

The existing Hungarian nationality law dates from 1993. Prior to this date, rules for acquisition and loss of Hungarian citizenship may have been different. With the new Hungarian nationality law, by January 2011, every person who was a Hungarian citizen or is a descendant of a person who was a Hungarian citizen before 1920, and speaks Hungarian may apply to become a Hungarian citizen even if he or she does not live in Hungary. As of July 22, 2011, more than 120,000 applications have been filed and 20,000 people have been granted citizenship thanks to the new nationality law. These people are mostly from Transylvania (Romania), Vojvodina (Serbia) and Ukraine.[66]

Dual citizenship is permitted under Hungarian law.

Citizenship by birth and adoption

A person acquires Hungarian citizenship at birth if at least one parent is a Hungarian citizen. The place of birth is irrelevant.

Children born in Hungary to foreign parents do not acquire Hungarian citizenship at birth unless they would otherwise be stateless.

Minor children adopted by Hungarian citizens may normally be granted Hungarian citizenship.

Naturalization as a Hungarian citizen

A person may be naturalized as a Hungarian citizen on the basis of the following requirements:

---

[66] "Hungary citizenship law triggers row with Slovakia." Reuters. Retrieved 2012-04-20.

- 8 years continuous residence in Hungary

- no criminal past

- a stable livelihood

- good character

- passing a test in basic constitutional studies.

The residence requirement is reduced to 3 years for:

- spouses of Hungarian citizens who have been married for three years (or who are widows or widowers).

- parents of Hungarian citizen minor children

- persons adopted by Hungarian citizens

- recognized refugees

The 2011 Hungarian Citizenship law allows all ethnic Hungarians to apply for simplified naturalization if they are able to prove knowledge of the Hungarian Language and provide evidence that he or she does indeed have Hungarian ancestry.

A 5 year residence requirement applies to a person who is:

- born in Hungary; or

- established residence in Hungary before age 18; or

- is stateless

Applicants aged 65 or over, those of diminished capacity, and persons holding a Hungarian language diploma (from a Hungarian institution) may be exempted the constitutional studies requirement.

Hungarian citizenship by declaration

Declaration is a simplified form of naturalization. The following people may be eligible to acquire Hungarian citizenship by declaration:

- persons who lost Hungarian citizenship through emigration between 15 September 1947 and 2 May 1990.

- Stateless persons aged less than 19, born in Hungary and residing in Hungary for the 5 years prior to the declaration.

Oath of allegiance

Persons becoming naturalized Hungarian citizens are expected to take an Oath of Allegiance as follows:

"I, (name), do solemnly promise that I shall consider Hungary my country. I shall be a loyal citizen of the Republic of Hungary, and shall honor and observe the Constitution and laws thereof. I shall defend my country as far as my strength allows, and shall serve it according to the best of my abilities allow."

Those who prefer may take an equivalent solemn promise instead of an oath.

Loss of Hungarian citizenship

It is not possible for a person to lose Hungarian citizenship involuntarily. The exception concerns fraudulent applications for naturalization (subject to a 10- year time bar after which action cannot be taken).

Hungarian citizens who hold another nationality and live outside Hungary may renounce their Hungarian citizenship.

Citizenship of the European Union

Hungarian citizens are also citizens of the European Union and thus enjoy rights of free movement and have the right to vote in elections for the European Parliament.

ITALY

*Italy is a unitary parliamentary republic in Southern Europe. To the
north, it borders France, Switzerland, Austria, and Slovenia along the
Alps. To the south, it consists of the entirety of the Italian Peninsula,
Sicily, Sardinia–the two largest islands in the Mediterranean Sea–and
many other smaller islands. The independent states of San Marino and
the Vatican City are enclaves within Italy, while Campione d'Italia is an
Italian exclave in Switzerland. Italy had a pre WWII Jewish population of
approximately 44,500, of which approximately 7,680 were murdered
during the Holocaust.*

- Jus sanguinis – An ancestor from Italy.
- Dual citizenship permitted

Possibly alone in this respect, Italian nationality law bestows citizenship
jure sanguinis. There is no limit of generations for the citizenship via
blood, but the Italian ancestor born in Italian territories before 1861 had

to die after 1861 anywhere in the world without losing the Italian citizenship before death to being able to continue the jure sanguinis chain. This is required because 1861 is the year that the Unification of the Italian territory took place. Another constraint is that each descendant of the ancestor through whom citizenship is claimed jure sanguinis can pass on citizenship only if the descendant was a citizen at the time of the birth of the person to whom they are passing it. So, if any person in the chain renounces or otherwise loses the Italian citizenship and then has a child, that child is not an Italian citizen jure sanguinis. A further constraint is that until January 1, 1948, Italian law did not permit women to pass on citizenship. Persons born before that date are not Italian citizens jure sanguinis if their line of descent from an Italian citizen depends on a female at some point before 1948.

According to Italian law, **multiple citizenship** is explicitly permitted under certain conditions if acquired on or after 15 August 1992. (Prior to that date, Italian citizens with jus soli citizenship elsewhere could keep their dual citizenship perpetually, but Italian citizenship was generally lost if a new citizenship was acquired, and the possibility of its loss through a new citizenship acquisition was subject to a few exceptions.) Those who acquired another citizenship after that date but before 23 January 2001 had three months to inform their local records office or the Italian consulate in their country of residence. Failure to do so carried a fine. Those who acquired another citizenship on or after 23 January 2001 could send an auto-declaration of acquisition of a foreign citizenship by post to the Italian consulate in their country of residence. On or after 31 March 2001, notification of any kind is no longer necessary.

Citizenship of the European Union

Italian citizens are also citizens of the European Union and thus enjoy rights of free movement and have the right to vote in elections for the European Parliament.

Italy's current citizenship laws

Law no. 91 of 1992[67]

Law number 91, passed on 5 February 1992, establishes that the following persons are citizens by birth:

a) The child of a citizen father or mother. b) Whoever is born within the Republic's territory if both parents are stateless or unknown, or if the child's citizenship does not follow that of the parents, pursuant to the law of their country. (article 1, first paragraph). By paragraph 2, foundlings recovered in Italy are citizens by birth if it cannot be proven that these persons are in possession of another citizenship. Article 3 partially restates the text contained in article 5 of law 123 of 1983 where it establishes that an adoptive child of an Italian citizen is Italian, even if the child is of foreign origin, and even if the child was born before the passing of the law. It has expressly established retroactivity in this situation.

This is notwithstanding the fact that the law otherwise precludes its own retroactive application in article 20, which provides that "...except as expressly provided, the citizenship status acquired prior to the present law is not altered, unless by events after its date of entry into force."

This provision, in concert with opinion number 105 of 15 April 1983, has provided that children of an Italian citizen mother and an alien father born before 1 January 1948 (date of the republican constitution's entry into force) remain subject to the old law 555 of 13 June 1912, despite the Constitutional Court's pronouncement of unconstitutionality in decision 30 of 1983.

Additionally law 91 of 1992 allows the possession of multiple citizenship, previously prohibited in article 5 of law 123 of 1983 for those Italians acquiring a new citizenship. This allowance of keeping

---

[67] "Law 91 of 1992 with amendments through July of 2009 (English)."European Union Observatory on Democracy (EUDO) - Citizenship. Retrieved 03 October 2012.

Italian citizenship is not applicable in all cases of an Italian acquiring foreign citizenship, because Italy has maintained treaties with some states to the effect that an Italian naturalizing in one of those states could lose Italian citizenship automatically. Law 91 of 1992 leaves those agreements in effect. (article 26)

Laws coming after 1992 have altered access to citizenship extending it to some categories of citizens who for historical reasons, in connection with war events, were still excluded.

These more recent laws follow:

1) Law no. 379 of 14 December 2000 "Provisions for the recognition of Italian citizenship for the persons born and resident in the territories belonging to the Austro-Hungarian Empire and their descendants". (Published in the Official Gazette no. 295 on 19 December 2000)

Law 379/2000 contained provisions to recognize Italian citizenship for those persons who were born and residing in Italy's annexed territories from the Austro-Hungarian Empire prior to 15 July 1920. The recognition was available also to their descendants. Recognition of Italian citizenship under law 379/2000 was given only to applicants, and the provisions expired in December of 2010.

2) Law no. 124 of March 2006 "Changes to law number 91 of 5 February 1992 concerning the recognition of Italian citizenship for nationals of Istria, Fiume, and Dalmatia and their descendants". (Published in the Official Gazette no. 73 on 28 March 2006)

Law 124/2006 allows individuals who were Italian citizens residing in territories ceded from Italy to Yugoslavia at the time of their cession to reclaim Italian citizen status. It gives the ability to claim Italian citizen status to those people with knowledge of Italian language and culture who are lineal descendants of the eligible persons who were residing in those regions.

In more recent times, reforms to the citizenship law favoring immigrants from outside of the European Union were discussed. These immigrants currently may apply for citizenship after the completion of ten years of residency in the territory of the republic.

Many aspects remain unresolved, such as the recognition of citizenship status for descendants of an Italian woman who before 1948 had married a foreign husband and lost Italian citizenship on account of her marriage. These cases have created a dual system for recognition of citizenship: While the descendants by a paternal line have no impediments to the recognition of their citizenship status - even if the ascendant emigrated in 1860 (before Italy formed a state); the descendants of an Italian woman - even if she was from the same family - today still find themselves precluded from reacquiring Italian citizenship, and their only possible remedy is to appear before an Italian judge.

LATVIA

Latvia is a country in the Baltic region of Northern Europe. It is bordered to the north by Estonia (border length 343 km), to the south by Lithuania (588 km), to the east by Russia (276 km), and to the southeast by Belarus (141 km), and it shares a maritime border to the west with Sweden. With 2,070,371 inhabitants (population of Latvia peaked at 2.67 million in 1990) and a territory of 64,589 km2 (24,938 sq. mi)[68] it is one of the least populous and least densely populated countries of the European Union. The capital of Latvia is Riga. The official language is Latvian and the currency is called Lats (Ls). The country has a temperate seasonal climate. Latvia had a pre WWII Jewish population of approximately 91,500, of which approximately 71,500 were murdered during the Holocaust. The actual murder rate on the territory of Latvia was approximately 90%. The numbers are skewed due to deportations of Jews by the Soviets into Siberia prior to the Nazi occupation.

- Jus sanguinis - Either parent is a citizen

---

[68]"Latvia in Brief." Latvian Institute. 2011. Retrieved 5 November 2011.

- Naturalization requirements may be waived for citizens or decedents thereof for Latvian, Lithuanian, or Polish citizens prior to 1940 or 1939 respectively

At the time of going to print, a new Citizenship law has been approved in Latvia, but not yet implemented. Please seek updated information here: http://www.am.gov.lv/en/service/consular-services/4727/

LITHUANIA

Lithuania is a country in Northern Europe, the largest of the three Baltic states. It is situated along the southeastern shore of the Baltic Sea, to the east of Sweden and Denmark. It borders Latvia to the north, Belarus to the east and south, Poland to the south, and Kaliningrad Oblast (a Russian exclave) to the southwest. Lithuania has an estimated population of 3 million as of 2012, and its capital and largest city is Vilnius. Lithuania (including Vilnius) had a pre WWII Jewish population of approximately 240,000, of which approximately 220,000 were murdered during the Holocaust. The actual murder rate on the territory of Lithuania was approximately 96.4%. The numbers are skewed due to deportations of Jews by the Soviets into Siberia prior to the Nazi occupation. Lithuania had the highest murder rate of Jews of any country in Europe.

- Jus sanguinis – Through citizenship up to a Great Grandparent.
- Dual citizenship limited.
- Children, grand and great-grandchildren of citizens of Lithuania from 1919 – 1940.

- Dual citizenship NOT allowed if ancestor left Lithuania AFTER 1940.

Lithuanian nationality law automatically grants citizenship to persons born within the current borders of Lithuania. Citizenship may also be granted by naturalization. Naturalization requires a residency period, an examination in the Lithuanian language, examination results demonstrating familiarity with the Lithuanian Constitution, a demonstrated means of support, and an oath of loyalty. A right of return clause was included in the 1991 constitution for persons who left Lithuania after its occupation by the Soviet Union in 1940 and their descendants.

In 1989, the legislature passed a nationality act granting automatic citizenship to those persons who could establish their own birth, or that of a parent or grandparent, within Lithuanian borders. Permanent residents not covered by these criteria were granted citizenship upon signing a loyalty oath. Language proficiency was not required. A 1991 treaty with Russia extended the definition of residency to those who had immigrated to Lithuania from Russia between 1989 and the ratification of the treaty. Subsequent applicants for citizenship were required to meet a set of naturalization standards, including Lithuanian language testing.

The citizenship requirements were the most liberal of those in the newly independent Baltic states. This is usually attributed to a relatively low level of immigration from other areas within the Soviet Union, resulting in a more ethnically homogenous population.[69]

In November 2006, the Constitutional Court of the Republic of Lithuania ruled that the Law on Citizenship (wording of 17 September 2002 with

---

[69] Dovile Budryte (2005). Taming nationalism?: political community building in the post-Soviet Baltic States. Ashgate Publishing, Ltd. p. 150. ISBN 978-0-7546-4281-7. Retrieved 11 February 2011.

subsequent amendments and supplements), was "controversial, inconsistent and confusing.". At issue was the possession of dual citizenship; the provision extended the right of citizenship, and hence the right to vote, to members of the post-Soviet Lithuanian diaspora, which was concentrated in the United States, Canada, Australia, and Argentina, and their children, grandchildren, and great-grandchildren. The most notable member of this diaspora was Lithuanian President Valdas Adamkus, who had become a United States citizen; he formally renounced US citizenship before taking the oath of office.

The petitioners held that basing citizenship on ethnic origin or nationality of the person violated the equality of persons and was discriminatory. The use and meaning of the term "repatriated" was especially controversial. The Lithuanian Seimas (parliament) passed a temporary law, expiring in 2010, which granted dual citizenship in exceptional cases, most notably to those who were Lithuanian citizens prior to 1940 and who fled during the Soviet occupations, as well as to their children and grandchildren. The text of the law, as of July 15, 2008, is listed at the Seimas website: Lithuanian citizenship laws (English translation).

During November 2010 the Seimas passed a law liberalizing dual citizenship requirements. President Dalia Grybauskaite vetoed it, stating that: "According to the Constitution, dual citizenship is a rare exception, not a common case."

Citizenship of the European Union

Lithuanian citizens are also citizens of the European Union and thus enjoy rights of free movement and have the right to vote in elections for the European Parliament.

MOLDOVA

Moldova is a landlocked nation in Eastern Europe located between Romania to the west and Ukraine to the north, east, and south. The capital city is Chișinău.

- Jus sanguinis – Descent from Grandparents
- Dual citizenship permitted in certain circumstances

CITIZENSHIP: Citizenship is based upon the Law of Citizenship, dated June 23, 1990. All who resided in the territory of Moldova before June 23, 1990, and have a viable means of support, may obtain citizenship automatically upon request.

BY BIRTH: Birth within the territory of Moldova does not automatically confer citizenship.

BY DESCENT: Child, at least one of whose parents is a citizen of Moldova, regardless of the child's country of birth.

REGISTRATION: Citizenship may be granted by registration for the following persons: Foreign national who has been married to a citizen of Moldova for at least three years. Child, 18 and under, who has been adopted by citizens of Moldova.

BY NATURALIZATION: Moldovan citizenship may be acquired upon fulfillment of the following conditions: Person must be at least 19 years old, have renounced previous citizenship, and have resided in the country for at least 10 years.

DUAL CITIZENSHIP: NOT RECOGNIZED. Exception: A foreign citizen can be granted Moldovan citizenship by Special Presidential Decree without renouncing former citizenship.

LOSS OF CITIZENSHIP:

VOLUNTARY: Voluntary renunciation of Moldovan citizenship is permitted by law. Contact the Embassy for details and required paperwork.

INVOLUNTARY: No information was provided. The Law on Citizenship states that Moldovan citizenship may be revoked for certain (unspecified) reasons.

THE NETHERLANDS

The Netherlands is a constituent country of the Kingdom of the Netherlands, consisting of twelve provinces in North-West Europe and three islands in the Caribbean. The European part of the Netherlands borders the North Sea to the north and west, Belgium to the south, and Germany to the east, and shares maritime borders with Belgium, Germany and the United Kingdom. It is a parliamentary democracy organized as a unitary state. The country capital is Amsterdam and the seat of government is The Hague.[70] The Netherlands in its entirety is often referred to as "Holland", although North and South Holland are actually only two of its provinces. The Netherlands had a pre WWII Jewish population of approximately 140,000, of which approximately 100,000 were murdered during the Holocaust.

- Jus sanguinis – Father was a citizen

- Goes back one parent

- Dual citizenship permitted in certain circumstances

---

[70]Dutch Ministry of Foreign affairs. "About the Nederlands." Retrieved 3 March 2011.

1.Is there a right to re-claim descent citizenship?

The Dutch Nationality Act (RWN) allows under certain circumstances former Dutch nationals to regain Dutch nationality through naturalization or option. Acquiring Dutch nationality through decent is only through a Dutch parent and before 01-01-1985 through a Dutch father.

2. If yes to #1, how many generations back does it go?

Only a Dutch parent and therefor only one generation

3. How does it apply to those born in ex Dutch colonies?

Within the Kingdom of the Netherlands nationality was ruled by only one Nationality Act.

At the time of gaining independence between the Netherlands and the independent countries a declaration was signed through which people remained Dutch or obtained the nationality from the independent state.

4. What are the usual procedures for someone to claim?

Obtaining proof that he/she was born from a Dutch parent

POLAND

Poland is a country in Central Europe, bordered by Germany to the west; the Czech Republic and Slovakia to the south; Ukraine, Belarus to the east; and the Baltic Sea and Kaliningrad Oblast, a Russian exclave, and Lithuania to the north. The total area of Poland is 312,679 square kilometers (120,726 sq. mi), making it the 69th largest country in the world and the 9th largest in Europe. [71] Poland has a population of over 38.5 million people, which makes it the 34th most populous country in the world and the sixth most populous member of the European Union, being its most populous post-communist member. Poland is a unitary state made up of 16 voivodeships. Poland had a pre WWII Jewish population of approximately 3,300,000, of which approximately 3,000,000 were murdered during the Holocaust.

- *Jus sanguinis – Ancestor was a citizen*

- *Those that left Poland for Israel between 1958-1984 lost citizenship, but are permitted to apply by declaration*

---

[71]"Concise Statistical Yearbook of Poland, 2008" (PDF).Central Statistical Office (Poland). 28 July 2008. Retrieved 2008-08-12.

- *Dual citizenship not explicitly recognized, but permitted*

Polish nationality law is based upon the principles of jus sanguinis. Children born to Polish parents usually acquire citizenship irrespective of place of birth. A person born in Poland to foreign parents does not normally become a Polish citizen.

Polish law does not deal with the issue of dual citizenship. Therefore Poland will view a dual citizen as if he or she was solely Polish. Thus, Poland does not recognize the foreign citizenship of its nationals when they are on Polish soil.

Citizenship by birth

A child born to a Polish parent is usually a Polish citizen at birth. This applies whether the child is born in Poland or elsewhere.

Young persons' resident and born in Poland

Polish citizenship may be acquired by notification or application by young persons who were born in Poland and hold a permanent resident permit in the following cases:

aged 18 or more and resident in Poland for five years (without parental permissions).

aged under 18 and resident in Poland for five years (only if parents acquired Polish citizenship before or at the same time when the child applies).

Citizenship by Naturalization

As of 15 August 2012, the Polish President may grant Polish citizenship to any foreigner, regardless of how long they have stayed in Poland. The new law will permit the President to grant citizenship who have lived in Poland for less than 5 years, or have not even lived there at all. This new law also moves away from renouncing foreign citizenship to apply for

Polish citizenship.

As of 15 August, there has been a change in the rules under which a government official will consider a foreigner as a Polish citizen. Before 15 August, the governor only acknowledged citizenship to those with undetermined citizenship of foreigners and stateless persons residing in Poland for at least five years, on the basis of a permanent residence permit. The new act will extend the recognition of citizenship to all foreigners who: reside in Poland for at least 3 years on the basis of a permanent residence permit, have a regular income and legal title to the apartment, and also know the Polish language. A language test may be administered to check for linguistic fluency.

The new law maintains two principles: the continuity, and the exclusivity of Polish citizenship. The first principle is that those who acquired Polish citizenship under the previous rules (before August 15), keep it. People who have been granted Polish citizenship on the basis of the previous rules, will keep them, provided that in the meantime, they do not lose them.

The Act has also been confirmed by the exclusivity of Polish citizenship. It means that a Polish citizen at the same time may have Polish citizenship and citizenship of another country. The new law on citizenship means that a person applying for the grant Polish citizenship renounced his citizenship.

Polish Citizenship Act also sets out ways of acquiring Polish citizenship: by law, i.e. by birth, finding the territory of Poland, adoption and repatriation, by granting the Polish citizenship, the recognition of a Polish citizen and the restoration of Polish citizenship.

The new law regulates different mode than previously recognized as a Polish citizen. Up to 15 August, a Polish citizen can only apply if they were a stateless person, a spouse of a Polish citizen or from Polish-blood descent. As of 15 August, Polish citizenship may apply to any foreigner who resides in Poland long-term, integrates into the society, know the Polish language, have housing, respect Polish law and does not pose as a threat to the national security. Polish citizenship can also be acquired on the basis of specific authorization, refugees, stateless persons, children and spouses of Polish citizens and persons of Polish origin. Also new, is the introduction of a standard form certificate for the recognition as a Polish citizen, granted by the Minister of Interior. The decision on the recognition of a foreigner as a Polish citizen will depend on the government. Furthermore, foreigners unhappy with the decision may appeal to the Minister of Interior.

Citizenship by descent

Citizenship can generally be claimed only by descendants of Polish citizens who left Poland after the country became an independent state in 1918. Also, there can be no break in Polish citizenship between the emigrant ancestor and the descendant. If the applicant's ancestor lost Polish citizenship, such as by becoming a citizen of another country before 1951, the descendant did not inherit Polish citizenship through that ancestor.

Polish migrants before 1962

Special rules exist concerning the acquisition and loss of Polish citizenship before 1962:

Between 1918 and 1951, acquisition of another citizenship caused the loss of Polish citizenship. Polish citizenship was also lost through service in another country's military or acceptance of a "public office" in another country.

In 1951Poland revoked its citizenship for all inhabitants (including ethnic Poles) of the former Polish territories east of the Curzon line that had been annexed by the Soviet Union in 1945. Those individuals had been naturalized as Soviet citizens and later, after the dissolution of the Soviet Union in 1991, acquired the citizenship of one of the resulting countries: Belarus, Ukraine, Lithuania, Latvia, Estonia, or Russia. Polish citizenship was also revoked for citizens of Germany who were residing outside Poland, unless they had a Polish spouse who was resident in Poland.

Polish citizens who emigrated to Israel between 1958 and 1984, and who normally became Israeli citizens on arrival (based on the Israeli "Law of Return" for those of Jewish descent), lost Polish citizenship automatically. They and their descendants may be eligible to acquire Polish citizenship by declaration.

Loss of Polish citizenship

Since 1962, Polish law (including the Constitution) does not allow the government to revoke someone's citizenship. Renunciation of Polish citizenship requires a petition with extensive supporting documentation subject to the approval of the President of Poland. Administrative processing of the petition can take up to several years and the President's decision is final and cannot be appealed in court.

Starting in 1968, the former communist regime initiated an anti-Semitic campaign that forced out of Poland from 15,000 to 20,000 Polish Jews, who were stripped of their Polish citizenship.

Their Polish passports confiscated, replaced with a 'travel document' that did not allow them to return., and their properties expropriated by the state, the mostly Holocaust survivors and their children emigrated to Israel, the United States, Denmark and Sweden.

The High Court in Warsaw accepted a petition filed by Baruch-Natan Yagil, who was forced to leave Poland in 1968, and ruled that the Polish government erred in revoking the plaintiff's citizenship, and should restore it, and issue him a Polish passport.

During a 2006 visit to Israel, President Lech Kaczynski promised to restore Polish citizenship. No blanket legislation covering the issue exists, but Jews and Israelis who were invited to Warsaw to mark the

40th anniversary of Poland's purging of the Jews on March 8, 1968, will be given back the Polish citizenship.

Dual citizenship

Polish law does not explicitly allow dual citizenship, but possession of another citizenship is tolerated since there are no penalties for its possession alone. However, penalties do exist for exercising foreign citizenship, such as identifying oneself to Polish authorities using a foreign identification document or serving in a foreign military without permission of Polish military authorities.

Poland treats nationals of other countries whom it considers Polish citizens as if they were solely Polish. Because Polish citizenship is determined by the citizenship of a Polish parent - without any explicit limitation for the number of generations elapsed abroad for descendants of Polish emigrants - this may create problems for individuals of Polish descent born abroad who, in spite of having no ties to Poland, are nevertheless subject to all obligations of Polish citizenship, formerly including military service (Poland suspended compulsory military service on December 5, 2008 by the order of the Minister of Defense and compulsory military service was formally abolished when the Polish parliament amended conscription law on January 9, 2009; the law came into effect on February 11.). In addition, such individuals are not entitled to consular protection of their home country under Article 29 of the Vienna Convention on Consular Relations. The only exception is when a bilateral consular agreement calls for recognition of the expatriate citizenship, regardless of the allegations of Polish citizenship raised by Poland. Such an agreement was negotiated in the 1972 Consular Convention between the United States and Poland providing that:

"Persons entering the Republic of Poland for temporary visits on the basis of United States passports containing Polish entry visas will, in the period for which temporary visitor status has been accorded (in conformity with the visa's validity), be considered United States citizens

by the appropriate Polish authorities for the purpose of ensuring the consular protection provided for in Article 29 of the Convention and the right of departure without further documentation, regardless of whether they may possess the citizenship of the Republic of Poland."

However, since Poland abolished visa requirements for United States citizens in 1991, this provision no longer applies.

The problems resulting for members of the Polish diaspora, Polonia, from being treated by Poland solely as Polish citizens are compounded by the difficulty to renounce Polish citizenship.

Poland has been enforcing with varying stringency its claims to citizenship allegiance from descendants of Polish emigrants and from recent refugees from Polish Communism who became naturalized in other countries. Under a particularly strict enforcement policy, named by the Polish expatriate community the "passport trap", citizens of the United States, Canada, and Australia were prevented from leaving Poland until they obtain a Polish passport. The governments of the United States and Canada have issued travel warnings for Poland, still in effect in February 2007, to those "who are or can be claimed as Polish citizens" that they are required to "enter and exit Poland on a Polish passport" and will not be "allowed to leave Poland until a new Polish passport has been obtained".

Traveler's to Poland who have Polish ancestors are advised to obtain in writing a statement from a Polish Consulate as to whether or not they will face any obligations in Poland, such as military service, taxation, or the requirement to obtain a Polish passport.

In December 2007 Poland established a Polish Charter which can grant some rights of Polish citizenship to people of Polish descent who do not have Polish citizenship and who reside in ex-USSR.

Citizenship of the European Union

Polish citizens are also citizens of the European Union and thus enjoy rights of free movement and have the right to vote in elections for the European Parliament.

PORTUGAL

Portugal is a country located in Southwestern Europe, on the Iberian Peninsula. It is the westernmost country of mainland Europe, and is bordered by the Atlantic Ocean to the west and south and by Spain to the north and east. Apart from continental Portugal, the Portuguese Republic holds sovereignty over the Atlantic archipelagos of Azores and Madeira, which are autonomous regions of Portugal. The country is named after its second largest city, Porto, whose Latin name was Portus Cale.

- Jus sanguinis – Descent from Grandparents
- Jus soli under limited circumstances
- Citizenship rights for Sephardic Jews under debate.
- Dual citizenship permitted

Portuguese nationality law is the legal set of rules that regulate access to Portuguese citizenship, which is acquired mainly through descent from a Portuguese parent, naturalization in Portugal or marriage to a Portuguese citizen.

In some cases, children born in Portugal to non-citizens may be eligible for Portuguese citizenship. However this does not apply to children born to tourists or short-term visitors. Portuguese citizenship law is complicated by the existence of numerous former colonies and in some cases it is possible to claim Portuguese citizenship by connection with one of these jurisdictions.

Overall the present Portuguese nationality law, dated from 1981, privileges Jus sanguinis, while the precedent law, of 1959, was based on the principle of Jus soli. This shift occurred in 1975 and 1981, thus basically making it difficult to access naturalization not only to first generation migrants, but also to their children and grandchildren. Only very recently, in 2006, was this situation slightly changed, but still stressing Jus sanguinis.

Birth in Portugal

In general a child born in Portugal to foreign parents is not entitled to Portuguese citizenship unless the parents have lived in Portugal for 6 years with valid residence permits.

Descent from a Portuguese parent

A child born to a Portuguese parent is automatically a Portuguese citizen provided the parent was born in Portugal or is employed by the Portuguese state. Or, the child may be registered as a Portuguese citizen.

Prior to 30 October 1981, there were a few restrictions on claiming Portuguese citizenship based on having a Portuguese mother only.

Naturalization as a Portuguese citizen

A person aged 18 or over may be naturalized as a Portuguese citizen after 6 years residence.[72] There is a requirement to have sufficient knowledge of the Portuguese language and effective links to the national community. Children aged under 18 may acquire Portuguese

---

[72]http://www.sef.pt/portal/v10/EN/aspx/noticias/Noticias_Detalhe.aspx?id_linha =4628

citizenship by declaration when a parent is naturalized.

Portuguese citizenship by adoption

A child adopted by a Portuguese citizen acquires Portuguese citizenship. Child should be under 18.

Portuguese citizenship by marriage

A person married to a Portuguese citizen for at least three years may be able to acquire Portuguese citizenship by declaration. No formal residence period in Portugal is laid down; however, in practice, knowledge of the Portuguese language and integration into Portuguese society may be required.

Portuguese citizenship for Jews

Effective July 2013, Portugal will offer Citizenship to Jewish descendants of Jews expelled during the Inquisition of 1536.

Dual citizenship

Portugal allows dual citizenship. Hence, Portuguese citizens holding or acquiring a foreign citizenship do not lose Portuguese citizenship. Similarly, those becoming Portuguese citizens do not have to renounce their foreign citizenship.

Although Portugal allows dual citizenship, some countries, such as Japan, do not. Thus, dual Portuguese–Japanese citizens, under Japanese nationality law, must declare to the Government of Japan whether they are going to keep their Japanese or Portuguese citizenship. A similar procedure has been required in past years for dual Portuguese–South Korean citizens. However, since 2011, South Korea has allowed dual citizenship for some categories of persons. See the South Korean nationality law article for more information.

Citizenship of the European Union

Portuguese citizens are also citizens of the European Union and thus enjoy rights of free movement and have the right to vote in elections for the European Parliament.

ROMANIA

Romania is a country located at the intersection of Central and Southeastern Europe (or the Balkan region), bordering on the Black Sea. Romania shares a border with Hungary and Serbia to the west, Ukraine and Moldova to the northeast and east, and Bulgaria to the south. At 238,400 square kilometers (92,000 sq. mi), Romania is the eighth largest country of the European Union by area, and has the seventh largest population of the European Union with more than 19 million people. Its capital and biggest city is Bucharest, the 11th largest city in the EU. Romania had a pre WWII Jewish population of approximately 609,000, of which approximately 280,000 were murdered during the Holocaust.

- Jus sanguinis – Up to Great-Grandparent
- Dual citizenship permitted

Romanian nationality law is based on the 1991 Romanian Citizenship law. It is based on the social policy of jus sanguinis (or "right of blood"), by which nationality or citizenship is not determined by place of birth, but by having an ancestor who is a national or citizen of the state. It contrasts with jus soli ("right of soil"). It does contain an element of jus soli in respect to foundlings: foundlings who are found in Romania are considered Romanian citizens until proven otherwise.[73]

The law

From Law 21, Art. 5.[74] – The children born from Romanian citizens on Romanian territory are Romanian citizens.

Furthermore, Romanian citizens are also those:

a) born on the Romanian territory, even if only one of the parents is a Romanian citizen;

b) born abroad and both parents, or only one of them has a Romanian citizenship.

The child found on Romanian territory is a Romanian citizen if none of the parents is known.

Romanian citizenship can also be acquired after 5 years of residence in the country and with a good knowledge of the Romanian language and culture.

The consequences of naturalization and restoration of Romanian nationality

Art. 10 of the Romanian nationality law stipulates "Romanian nationality can be granted to the person who lost this nationality and requests its restoration, keeping his/her foreign nationality..." But having in mind that certain countries do not allow for multiple citizenship or, in the case that they do allow it, they provide for automatic loss of their citizenship at obtaining the nationality of another country through a voluntary decision (free choice), the Romanian state cannot guarantee that the foreign citizen keeps his/her foreign citizenship when restoring

---

[73] Art. 5 of the Romanian nationality law, Law no. 21/1991 republished in 2010.
[74] Ministry of Justice - Law on Romanian Citizenship (in Romanian, English and French)

his/her Romanian nationality. E.g. a Belgian subject who restored his/her Romanian nationality before 9 June 2007 has ceased to be a Belgian subject since restoring his/her Romanian citizenship. The same applies to a Dutch subject who restored his/her Romanian nationality before 1 April 2003, as well as for a Dutch subject who has restored his/her Romanian nationality after 1 April 2003, but does not fulfill at least one of the three exceptions from automatically losing his/her Dutch nationality when voluntarily obtaining another nationality. This does not constitute a fault of the Romanian state, since "according to the Romanian Constitution and Art. 1, paragraph 3 of Law No. 21 of 1991 with the subsequent changes and additions, republished, the nationals of Romania enjoy the protection of the Romanian state — such provisions do not mention any duty of the Romanian state in respect to former and/or future Romanian nationals".

The same applies to people who get naturalized as Romanian nationals.

Citizenship of the European Union

Romanian citizens are also citizens of the European Union and thus enjoy rights of free movement and have the right to vote in elections for the European Parliament.

RUSSIA

Russia is a federal semi-presidential republic, comprising 83 federal subjects. From northwest to southeast, Russia shares land borders with Norway, Finland, Estonia, Latvia, Lithuania and Poland (both with Kaliningrad Oblast), Belarus, Ukraine, Georgia, Azerbaijan, Kazakhstan, China, Mongolia, and North Korea. It shares maritime borders with Japan by the Sea of Okhotsk, and the U.S. state of Alaska across the Bering Strait. At 17,075,400 square kilometers (6,592,800 sq. mi), Russia is the largest country in the world, covering more than one-eighth of the Earth's inhabited land area. Russia is also the world's ninth most populous nation with 143 million people as of 2012. Extending across the whole of northern Asia, Russia spans nine time zones and incorporates a wide range of environments and landform. Russia (in this case the countries of the FSU – i.e. including Ukraine and Belarus) had a pre WWII Jewish population of approximately 3,000,000, of which approximately 1,100,000 were murdered during the Holocaust.

- Jus sanguinis - Either parent is a citizen

- Residents of various former USSR states can become Russian citizens through various means

- Dual citizenship permitted with certain countries

In 2002, a new citizenship act, supported by President Putin, replaced the act of 1991.

Russian citizenship could be acquired:

- by birth
- by naturalization
- by restoration of citizenship
- by following parents' citizenship

The rules of citizenship by birth generally follow the principle of jus sanguinis, though a child can be recognized as a Russian citizen in several special cases:

- neither parent, both of whom are permanent residents of Russia, is a Russian citizen, but the child is born in Russia and does not acquire any other citizenship
- the child is found abandoned on Russian territory and the parents remain unknown for more than six months

Naturalization is usually granted if the applicant meets the following requirements:

- has been a permanent resident of Russia for not less than five years
- promises lawful behavior
- has a legal source of income
- has applied for termination of another citizenship (though the actual loss of foreign citizenship is not required)
- speaks Russian

In certain cases some or even all of the above requirements can be waived. Restoration of citizenship is granted under the same rules as naturalization; the only exception is the residence term requirement (three years in this case). Although not in compliance with law, executive agencies (such as the federal migration service and Russian diplomatic and consular departments abroad) usually do not grant Russian citizenship to former Russian citizens if they do not satisfy citizenship restoration requirements, even if they satisfy requirements for facilitated naturalization.

A special provision of law made it possible for former citizens of the USSR to apply for Russian citizenship before 2009. The only requirements were holding a temporary residence permit or a permanent residence permit, or being registered as a permanent resident of Russia as of July 1, 2002 and meeting the naturalization requirements of p. 2 and p. 4.

Citizenship of children (persons under 18 years of age) generally follows the citizenship of their parents. If one or both parents obtain Russian citizenship, their children become Russian citizens as well. If one or both parents lose Russian citizenship, their children lose it too. A child can acquire or relinquish Russian citizenship by the application of his parents, but at least one parent must be a Russian citizen in this case.

Eurasian Economic Community treaties

The Russian Federation has a treaty with Kazakhstan and a treaty with Kyrgyzstan. There is also a multilateral treaty among the Russian Federation, Kazakhstan, Kyrgyzstan and the Republic of Belarus.

Citizens of the respective states that come to Russia for permanent residence have the right to obtain Russian citizenship if they: were citizens of the RSFSR, or were born in the territory of the RSFSR, or were living in the territory of the RSFSR before December 21, 1991, or have relatives who are citizens or permanent residents of the Russian Federation.

Until the end of 2003, those treaties were ignored by Russian executive authorities.[75] Presidential Decree N 1545 provided some means for

---

[75] "Declaration of State Duma on citizenship issues." Wbase.duma.gov.ru. Retrieved 2012-11-18.

implementation of the treaties. However, the decree requires that the applicant provide evidence that the state of his citizenship allows him to reside in Russia (such as a special stamp in a passport or an exit document). This does not conform to the treaties and makes obtaining citizenship significantly more difficult or even impossible in some cases. The Supreme Court of the Russian Federation stated in its decision that one must prove, in accordance with the treaties, that he came to Russia for permanent and not temporary residence. This can be proved in accordance with Russian law. In accordance with the Act on the Status of Foreign Citizens in the Russian Federation, obtaining temporary or permanent residence permission in Russia does not require any permission from foreign states, so technically every person who lawfully resides in Russia is able to apply for a temporary residence permit and then for a permanent residence permit. Although the interpretation of the Federal Act given by the Supreme Court is incompatible with the Presidential Decree, the article was not declared void.

Dual citizenship treaties

The following international treaties contain rules related to dual citizenship:

Treaty between the Russian Federation and the Republic of Tajikistan (1995)

Treaty between the Russian Federation and the Republic of Turkmenistan (1993), the current status of which is in dispute

The Treaty of Friendship, Cooperation, and Mutual Security between the Russian Federation and the Republic of Armenia, signed December 29, 1991, grants the right to acquire citizenship of both Russia and Armenia to the citizens of Russia and Armenia.

As the Russian Federation is the successor state to the Soviet Union, some Soviet treaties on dual citizenship are still in force. For this reason, the Convention on the Nationality of Married Women is in force.

European Convention on Nationality

The European Convention on Nationality has been signed but not ratified by the Russian Federation. It is binding to the extent of the provisions of the Vienna Convention on International Treaties. Domestic citizenship legislation is usually considered to conform to the convention.

SPAIN

Spain is a sovereign state and a member of the European Union. It is located on the Iberian Peninsula in southwestern Europe. Its mainland is bordered to the south and east by the Mediterranean Sea except for a small land boundary with Gibraltar; to the north and north east by France, Andorra, and the Bay of Biscay; and to the west and northwest by Portugal and the Atlantic Ocean. The border with Spain (1,214 km long) is the longest uninterrupted border within the European Union.

- Jus sanguinis - Either parent is a citizen

- Jus soli under limited circumstances

- Sephardic Jews residency requirement removed, streamlining dual citizenship

- Decedants of Spanish Civil War that were exiled permitted to apply for citizenship

- Dual citizenship permitted for those originating as Spanish citizens

Dual nationality

Dual citizenship is permitted for all Spaniards by origin, as long as they declare their will to retain the Spanish nationality within three years of the acquisition of another nationality. This requirement is waived for those individuals who are natural citizens of an Iberoamerican country, Andorra, the Philippines, Equatorial Guinea or Portugal, and any other country that Spain may sign a bilateral agreement with.

On the other hand, foreign nationals that acquire the Spanish nationality lose their previous nationality, unless they were natural born citizens of an Iberoamerican country, Andorra, the Philippines, Equatorial Guinea or Portugal, even if these countries do not grant their citizens a similar treatment.

Citizenship of the European Union

Spanish citizens are also citizens of the European Union and thus enjoy rights of free movement and have the right to vote in elections for the European Parliament.

Spanish nationality by origin

Spanish legislation regarding nationality establishes two types of nationality: "Spanish nationality by origin" (nacionalidad española de origen, in Spanish)—that is, a "natural-born Spaniard"—and the "Spanish nationality not by origin" (nacionalidad española no de origen in Spanish).

According to article 17 of the Spanish Civil Code, Spaniards by origin are:

- those individuals born of a Spanish parent;

- those individuals born in Spain of foreign parents if at least one of the parents was also born in Spain, with the exception of children of foreign diplomatic or consular officers accredited in Spain;

- those individuals born in Spain of foreign parents if neither of them have a nationality, or if the legislation of either parent's home country does not grant the child any nationality;

- those individuals born in Spain of undetermined filiation; those individuals whose first known territory of residence is Spain, are considered born in Spain.

Foreigners under 18 years of age who are adopted by a Spanish national acquire, from the moment of adoption, Spanish nationality by origin.[76] If the adoptee is 18 years or older, he or she can apply (lit. "opt") for Spanish nationality by origin within two years after the adoption took place.

All other individuals that acquire Spanish nationality, other than by which is specified above, are "Spaniards not by origin".

Spanish nationality by option

Article 20 of the Spanish Civil Code, established that the following individuals have the right to apply (lit. "to opt") for Spanish nationality:

- those individuals that were under the tutelage of a Spanish citizen,

- those individuals whose father or mother had been originally Spanish and born in Spain (i.e. those individuals who were born after their parent(s) had lost Spanish nationality).

- those individuals mentioned in the second bullet-point in article 17, and adopted foreigners of 18 years of age or more.

Spanish nationality by naturalization and residence

Spanish nationality can be acquired by naturalization, which is given only at the discretion of the government through a Royal Decree, and under exceptional circumstances.[77] Any individual can request the Spanish nationality by naturalization, as long as he or she is 18 years or older, or through a legal representative if he or she is younger.

Spanish nationality can also be acquired by residence in Spain. To apply for naturalization by residence it is necessary for the individual to have

---

[76]Artículo 17. Código Civil Español
[77]Carta de Naturaleza. MInisterio de Justicia.

lived in Spain for: ten years, or five years if the individual is a refugee, or two years if the individual is a national of a country of Iberoamerica, Andorra, Philippines, Equatorial Guinea, Portugal, or a Sephardi Jew or one year for those individuals:

- born in Spanish territory, or

- those who did not exercise their right to their nationality by option within the established period of time, or

- those who had been under legal tutelage or protection of a Spanish citizen or institution for two consecutive years,

- those who had been married for one year to a Spanish national and are not separated legally or de facto, or

- those widowers of a Spanish national if at the time of death they had not been legally or de facto separated, or

- those born outside of Spain, if one of their parents or grandparents had been originally Spanish (i.e. Spanish by origin).

Loss and recovery of Spanish nationality

Spanish nationality can be lost under the following circumstances:

Those individuals of 18 years of age or more whose residence is not Spain and who acquire voluntarily another nationality, or who use exclusively another nationality, which was conferred to them prior to their age of emancipation lose Spanish nationality. In this case, loss of nationality occurs three years after the acquisition of the foreign nationality or emancipation only if they individual does not declare their will to retain Spanish nationality. The exception to this are those Spaniards by origin who acquire the nationality of an Iberoamerican country, Andorra, Philippines, Equatorial Guinea or Portugal;

Those Spanish nationals that expressly renounce Spanish nationality if they also possess another nationality and reside outside Spain will lose Spanish nationality;

Those minors born outside Spain that have acquired Spanish

citizenship being children of Spanish nationals that were also born outside Spain, and if the laws of the country in which they live grant them another nationality, will lose Spanish nationality if they do not declare their will to retain it within three years after their 18th birthday or the date of their emancipation.

In addition, Spaniards "not by origin", will lose their nationality if:

- they use exclusively for a period of three years their previous nationality—with the exception of the nationality of those countries that Spain has signed an agreement of double nationality with;

- they participate voluntarily in the army of a foreign country, or serve in public office in a foreign government, against the specific prohibition of the Spanish government;

- they had lied or committed fraud when they applied for Spanish nationality.

Those individuals who had lost the Spanish nationality can recover it if they become legal residents in Spain. Nonetheless, emigrants and their children are not required to return to Spain to recover the Spanish nationality.

APPENDIX

Appendix 1:

Hearings in front of the USA Committee on Immigration and Naturalization in the House of Representatives, in the 64th Congress, First Session on H.R. 558 on Thursday, January 20, 1916, concerning Restriction of Immigration into USA. Pages 685-698:

RUSSIAN ATROCITIES AGAINST THE JEWS.

EXPULSION OF THE JEWS BY THE RUSSIAN GOVERNMENT DURNG THE PRESENT WAR

INTRODUCTORY.

Modern theory of international law condemns acts of cruelty or reprisals committed by the civil government or the army of a belligerent against noncombatant citizens of an enemy nation. Unfortunately neither side to the present war has lived up to this theoretical standard. But the Government of the Czar has offered the only example known to history of a government using a foreign war as a pretext for acts of wanton cruelty against its own unarmed and defenseless subjects.

EXPULSION OF THE RUSSIAN JEWS.

The Russian Government has inaugurated a campaign of extermination against the Jewish people. Not content with the traditional pogroms, the Government has resorted to general expulsion of the Jews from entire sections, which does not strike the imagination as much as does a pogrom, attended by violation of women and other fiendish deeds, but surpasses any and all pogroms in the devastation wrought by it.

Expulsion of the Jews has become an everyday occurrence. What seemed an impossibility, even in the land of the Tsar, quite appropriately named the "land of unlimited possibilities" has now become a reality. The expulsion of the Jews has assumed enormous proportions extending beyond the boundaries of Poland, to Lithuania and the Baltic region. The "Pale of Settlement," the section assigned to the Jews for habitation, has become the place of wandering for hundreds of thousands of people driven from town to town at the caprice of the authorities. Bureaucrats, who could not organize the war against the foreign enemy, have displayed amazing inventiveness and energy in organizing the war against their own unarmed people. In a few hours, or a few days at least, they depopulate entire cities and provinces, and, with the thoroughness of expert pogrom makers, they are turning into a desert a cultivated region linked by a thousand economic ties with the rest of Russia.

The expulsion of the Jews is intended as an excuse for the defeats suffered by the Russian Army. The soldiers and the masses are made to believe that the Russian defeats are due to the fact that the army has to operate in a section with an enormous Jewish population, which supplies the Germans with information concerning the disposition and movements of the Russian Army, furnishes them with supplies, etc. The expulsion of the Jews is but a method to give this calumny wide circulation.

The facts laid before the American public in the following pages have been compiled exclusively from Russian newspapers which have passed the scrutiny of the Russian military censor. A newspaper that would dare to circulate false or exaggerated reports of the acts of the Government at the present time would make itself table to severe punishment.

GRAND DUKE NICHOLAS NICHOLAYEVITCH ACCUSES THE JEWS OF GIVING AID TO THE ENEMY—HOSTAGES TAKEN FROM THE JEWISH POPULATION.

The headquarters from which the false charges of Jewish treason were issued was the general staff of the commander in chief, Grand Duke Nicholas Nicholayevitch. As early as in November of last year an army order was sent along the Polish front, in which soldiers were told that the Germans had met reliable allies in the Russian Jews who, in addition to furnishing them with supplies, are the best and often unselfish spies, ready to render any service which is likely to injure the Russian cause. It was therefore ordered to search for underground telephones and telegraphs, by means of which the Jews were alleged to communicate with the Germans, to take hostages from the Jewish population, and to execute those hostages "in case of treasonable activity on the part of any one of the local inhabitants."

GRAND DUKE ORDERS EXPULSION OF ALL JEWS.

The record of persecution was beaten by the last orders concocted in the tent of the commander in chief. The most remarkable of them all is the "manifesto" to the soldiers, which begins with the words, "The cup of patience has been filled to overflowing." The Jews, says the "manifesto," render services to the Germans, the army must be on the lookout against them in every way. For this reason a general order has been issued directing the expulsion of all Jews from the zone of military operations.

EXPULSION OF THE JEWS FROM POLISH TOWNS—OLD MEN, WOMEN, AND CHILDREN DRIVEN INTO THE COLD—MANY HAD TO WALK ALL THE WAY TO WARSAW.

Expulsion of the Jews, by the Russian military and civil authorities, closely followed the invasion of Russian territory by the German Army. The following description of the expulsion from Poland is given by a correspondent of the Retch, of which Prof. Paul Milukov, the leader of the Constitutional Democratic Party in the Duma, is the editor.

"On January 25 I was in Grodzisko and saw how the signal to leave was given to the Jews by tapping on the window panes from the street. Within a few minutes this anthill poured out into the streets and, shouting and crying, ran for the train. Some carried children, some their old folks, others carried bundles with some household effects. All platforms, all car buffers, finally all roofs were choked with people. It was a sort of living serpent made up of human bodies."

The picture of wholesale destruction of human beings rises before us in all its horrifying reality even from the censored press reports, of the arrival of the exiles in Warsaw;

"All last night and all of yesterday, through the streets of Warsaw stretched an endless stream of horsecarts packed with old folks, women, and children, shivering with cold and cuddling up to one another. Behind these walked the men folk, almost bent double, for whom there was no room in the carts. All night long the benumbed Jews wandered about the darkened streets of Warsaw, not knowing where to lay their wearied heads to rest, to whom to apply for aid. Ever and anon the silence of the night would be broken by the crying of the almost frozen and hungry infants and the moans of the women." * * * Only a very insignificant part of the enormous mass of the homeless were lucky enough to secure horsecarts or get on the train. The poorer folk, and in general those living away from the railway line, had to walk. These wanderers had to carry the children, the old, and the sick." [1]

The privations of the exiles grew worse, if worse they could be, when the authorities barred them from Warsaw, since anything like substantial assistance could be given them only in a great city with a large Jewish population. The Jews, expelled to the right bank of the Vistula, were compelled to spend two or three winter days in the open air, having nothing to cover their bodies with because they had been unable to take along anything of their belongings, owing to the suddenness and hurry of their departure.[2]

FOUR-FIFTHS OF THE POPULATION OF THE POLISH TOWNS EXPELLED.

The following summary of the expulsion policy in Poland is furnished by a Polish newspaper: "In the region where the Jews constituted over 80 per cent of the total population of the small towns, at present not a single Jew is to be found in those same towns situated within the zone of military operations."[3]

EXPELLED JEWS TREATED LIKE PRISONERS.

With the expulsion of the Jews from the Province of Suwalki, which is the connecting link between Poland and Lithuania, a new feature was put into practice; the expelled Jews were classed as prisoners, they were denied the right to choose a place of residence even within the limits of the pale of settlement,[4] and were supplied with "Certificates of passage" to specified districts, like suspicious characters;[5] in certain places they were convoyed by guards; in the larger towns situated on their route they were mostly refused admittance, even for the very briefest respite,[4] and if, through the oversight of the police, they happened to get in there, they were mercilessly driven farther.

1 Haint, January28, 1915.

2 The Jewish W eek, No. 1, May 24,1915.

3 Ziemia Lubelska, No. III, Apr. 23,1915.

4 See Appendix IV.

5 See Appendix, section7

ORDER OF EXPULSION EXTENDED TO LITHUANIA AND THE BALTIC PROVINCES.

In the latter part of April and early in May, 1915, expulsion of the Jews was ordered on an enormous scale extending over the whole area of the provinces of Grodno, Kovno, and Kurland. The entire "pale of Jewish settlement" was overflowed by the stream of exiles, running into hundreds of thousands.[1]

TEXT OFTHE ORDER FORTHE EXPULSION OF JEWS FROM KOWNO.

The Kowno administration received the following order from military headquarters: " Pursuant to the order of the commander in chief of the army, each and every Jew residing to the west of the line Kowno-Yanoff-Wilkomir-Rogoff-Ponyevezh-Posvol-Salata-Bausk shall be expelled. The points herein enumerated are likewise included within the territory from which the Jews shall be expelled. With regard to the Jews living within the territory at present occupied by the German forces, the said order shall be carried out immediately after the said territory is cleared of the enemy forces and upon its occupation by our troops. The expelled Jews must proceed to one of the following districts: Bakhmut, Mariupol and Slavyanoserbsk, of the Province of Yekaterinoslav, and Poltava, Gadyach, Zenkoff, Kobeiyaki, Konstantinograd, Lokhvitsa, Lubny, Mirgorod, Romny and Khorol of the Province of Poltava. The time limit for their departure has been set for the 5/18 of this May. After that date, sojourning of the Jews to the west of the said line will be punished in accordance with martial law, and the police officials failing to take effective measures for the enforcement of the said order will be removed from office and indicted. Notice of the foregoing hereby being given for enforcement, you are directed, upon the completion of the general expulsion of Jews beyond the said limit of the territory under your jurisdiction, to report to me by telegraph by 12 midnight of May 5. The progress of the expulsion of the Jews from territory now held by the enemy shall be reported as fast as the same is carried out."[2]

TWO DAYS' NOTICE TO QUIT.

In accordance with this order, the Jews were expelled from a number of districts of the Province of Kowno, viz: Kowno, Shavli, Ponyevyezh, Vilkomir, etc.[3]The expulsion was carried out with cruelty characteristic of the Russian bureaucracy. On Sunday, May 3/16, in the evening, the police gave notice to the Jewish inhabitants of the city of Kowno, that they must all leave the city not later than 12 o'clock at midnight, May 5/18. Nearly 20,000 Jews were expelled at one swoop.[4]

THREATENED WITH MARTIAL LAW IFTOO SLOW IN LEAVING.

On April 30/May 13, 1915, an order was promulgated for the expulsion of all Jews from the Province of Kurland on or before May 4/17, 1915. The Jews who would not leave voluntarily by May 4/17 would be deported with their families under guard, and, moreover, would be liable to prosecution under martial law.[6]

An unusual exception was made by the authorities of Mitau for a few Jews, viz, Dr. Feitelberg, who held the office of city physician, a few patients, and a butcher.[6]

The administration keenly watched that none of those who were expelled from Kurland should stay anywhere else in the Baltic region; those among them who had rushed to Riga during the early days were immediately forced to leave.[7]

BUSINESS OF THE COMMUNITY RUINED.

The Jews expelled from Mitau (the capital of Kurland) had lived there for many generations, and had grown deeply rooted in the life of the city. It goes without saying that the expulsion of the Jews dealt a powerful blow to the business life ofKurland.[7]

ORDER TO QUIT INSTANTER.

The administration did all in its power to aggravate the conditions of expulsion. The exiles from Kurland were allowed only from 5 to 24 hours to leave.[8] In Riga, the authorities ordered them to quit immediately, threatening that otherwise they would be deported under guard and that hostages would be taken from them. After extraordinary efforts, their time to leave was extended.[9]

1 See Appendix, I (b), (c), and (d)

2. Retch, May 10, 1915.

3 Retch, May 6/19

4 Retch, May 9,1915.

5 Retch, May 3,1915.

6 Kieff Thought, May 7/20, 1915

7 Retch, May 6, 1915

8 Jewish Week No. 4 1915

9 Jewish Week No. 3, 1915

EXILES DRIVEN PROM PILLAR TO POST.

To cap the misery of the exiles, in a number of localities they were ordered out again. Thus the exiles from the Provinces of Kovno and Kurland, were forbidden to stop off at Vilna.[1] Those of them who had already managed to get into Vilna were ordered, by the highest military authority, to be expelled from the city within 10 days.[2] In Warsaw the police gave notice to the exiles that they were not within any category of persons entitled to remain in Warsaw, by virtue of the order of the commander in chief, and that accordingly they must leave the city.[3]

NEVER TO RETURN TO THEIR HOMES.

That the expelled residents of Kovno might cherish no hopes ever to return to their homes, the administration ordered all the Jews to be struck off the registration books as no longer residing within the zone of the Kovno Fortress.[4]

HOSTAGES DEMANDED A CONDITION FOR RETURN OF THE EXILES.

The Kieff committee of relief to the Jews petitioned the governor of Kovno for leave to the Jewish exiles from the Province of Kovno to return home. The following telegram came in reply to this petition:

"The Jews deported from a part of the Province of Kovno beyond the line Riga-Bausk-Ponyevyezh-Vilkomir-Kovno may reside only beyond that line, to wit: in the Novo-Alexandrovsk district and part of the Vilkomir district, to the east of the above-mentioned line. Return to permanent residence, if within the zone of military operations, is allowed only on condition that acceptable hostages be first furnished.

"(Signed) **GOVERNOR GRYAZNOFF.**"

The Jews refused to avail themselves of this peculiar privilege.[6]

MEMBER OF THE DUMA BARRED FROM HIS DISTRICT.

Even Mr. Friedman, member of the Imperial Duma from the Province of Kovno, was not allowed to come to his home in Ponyevyezh to wind up his business.

A PEOPLE TURNED INTO PAUPERS.

In the rush with which the expulsion was carried out—within one or two days, at times only a few hours—no one could she any time to his business. Factories, stores, shops, house furnishings, personal belongings, everything, was left to fate. Deprived of the opportunity to take along with them even the most necessary of their belongings, the exiles suddenly found themselves in the condition of paupers sent out into the world to beg. "On many of them their underwear has been entirely worn out and turned into dirty rags." [6]

EXILES PACKED OFF IN CATTLE CARS—MANY FORCED TO WALK.

The semiservitude in which the Jewish masses are held in Russia has strikingly manifested itself in the manner of deportation of the exiles. They were transported in cattle cars, into which healthy and sick, men, women, and children were packed like sardines. Yet lucky were those who managed to get into a car of this kind, because enormous crowds had to travel on foot.

FAMILIES BROKEN UP—CHILDREN LOST.

With the expulsion of the Jews from the Province of Kovno, the whole "Pale of Settlement" was set a moving. Reading the newspaper reports, one might think that the times of the great migration had returned.

The chronicle of expulsion abounds in dramatic detail. In one train the body of a child was found; a paralyzed woman was discovered; a lunatic, and a 105-year-old woman were taken off a train.

An overwhelming impression is produced by the exceedingly long list of lost relatives which are published in the newspapers. In the turmoil accompanying the

1 Jewish Week. May 24, 1915.

2 Haint, May 18, 1915.

3 Haint, June 10. 1915.

4 Haint, May 20, 1915.

5 The War and The Jews. Weekly, 1915. No. 11.

6 The Jewish Week, No. 1, 1915.

Expulsion, which was carried out with dazing speed, hundreds of children, women, and old folks were lost. And so now one is looking for his children, another for his wife, another for his sisters, and still another for his parents.[1]

The number of lost exiles was so large that special information bureaus had to be established by the Vilna and Dvinsk Societies for the relief of the war sufferers,[2]

GOING INSANE FROM GRIEF OVER LOST FAMILIES.

The expulsion, the breaking up of families, produced numerous cases of mental derangement among the exiles, which threatened to become epidemic.[3]

NO SHELTER FOR THE EXILES—MANY MUST CAMP IN THE OPEN AIR.

The condition of the exiles became intolerable, owing to the fact that on reaching the left bank of the Dnyepr they were assigned to a limited number of small boroughs, in which thousands upon thousands of people congested, who simply could not find any shelter. In numerous cases the exiles had to camp in the open air.[4] As a rule, the Jewish exiles outnumbered the local Jewish population. But the exiles could not be distributed over rural settlements, owing to the regulations forbidding the Jews to settle outside of incorporated cities and towns.

CONGESTION OF EXILES FORCES THE GOVERNMENT TO SUSPEND THE STATUTES CONFINING THE JEWS TO A GHETTO.

All Russia proper was closed to the exiles by the statutes confining the Jews to a "pale of settlement." The overcrowding of the pale forced the Government to throw open to the exiles the Province of Voronyezh, outside the "pale of settlement," and late in August the Jews were permitted to settle beyond the pale.

MEN BATTLING AT THE FRONT, THEIR FAMILIES EXILED.

There is one striking detail in the chronicle of expulsions—the enormous preponderance of women, children, and old people, which at first glance seems incomprehensible, considering that the order of expulsion affects all Jews alike. The explanation, however, is simple: The men in most cases have been taken into the Army, and that at a rate considerably in excess of the ratio of Jews to the whole population of the Empire.

An illustration of this fact may be found in the results of an inquiry made by the Chernigoff committee for the relief of the Jewish population. It has investigated 139 exile families numbering 589 persons, who have come to Chernigoff from the zone of military operations, mostly from the Province of Kowno; 95 members of those families had gone to war. There were some exiled families who had two or three members on the fighting line.   On the average every 10 families had furnished 7 men to the army.[5]

MEN DEPORTED ON SUSPICION OF SPYING DRAFTED INTO THE ARMY.

In some cases Jewish young men subject to conscription were, after deportation returned to their former residences to be drafted into the army.[6]

Accordingly a Jew who has been deported from the zone of military operations on suspicion of sympathizing with the Germans is given access to that very army which it was intended to protect from a "blow in the back" by him. This hardly tallies with the legend of "Jewish treason," manufactured by the Government.

SIX HUNDRED THOUSAND DRIVEN FROM THEIR HOMES BY THE CZAR'SGOVERNMENT.

ALL STARVING.

The number of Jews deported from the northwestern region on a few days' notice is colossal.

At a conference of the Petrograd central committee for the relief of Jewish war sufferers last May in which representatives of the most prominent provincial committees participated, the total number of homeless Jews ruined by the expulsion in Poland and the northwestern section was conservatively figured at 600.000.[7]

1 See Appendix V.

2 The Jewish Week, No 3, 1913

3 See Appendix VI

4 Jewish Week, No 1, 1915

5 Kieff Thought, June 26,1915.

6 See Appendix VIII

7 Haint, May 21, 1915

This number comprises only those Jews who have not a penny to their names, who are in need of daily assistance of shelter and food, and many of them in need of the means necessary for traveling to the places assigned to them for residence. Tens of millions of roubles are wanted in order to save these masses barely from death through starvation.

THE WHOLE JEWISH PEOPLE BRANDED AS SPIES—NOT PERMITTED TO TRAVEL ONBUSINESS—NONRESIDENTS EXPELLED.

The condition of the Jews who were allowed to remain in the western section was likewise made unbearable. To say nothing of the fact that the Damocles sword of expulsion was hanging over them, paralyzing all their energy, by complete uncertainty of the morrow, the May orders of the commander in chief of the Russian Army, as interpreted and supplemented by the commanders of the northwestern and southwestern fronts, threatened to destroy all productive forces over an enormous area at their very roots.

By these orders, bearing the characteristic title: "Precautionary rules against spy emissaries," the millions of Jews living in this vast region were all suspected of spying. Communications between towns have been rendered difficult in the extreme. To enter such points as Kovno,

Grodno, Brest-Litovsk, Warsaw, Riga, Vilna, Byelostok, Rovno, Zhmerinka, etc., a special permit from proper military authority was required. Such permits were issued upon extremely oppressive terms, for a single passage and for brief periods. Only persons who had resided there prior to July 1/14, 1914.were allowed to stay there; all others had either to procure, from the military authorities, permits for further residence or to leave within 10 days.[1]

From Bialystok it was reported that orders had been given to expel immediately all clerical employees of mercantile establishments unless they had settled in that city prior to July 1/14, 1914.[2] The Birzhevyia Vyedomosti reported the expulsion from Riga of all persons who had settled in that place. * * *

[1] I consider it quite intolerable that a whole class of the population should be held under suspicion of espionage." [3] The convention instructed its council to make representations to the Government that the expulsion of the Jews from the Province of Kovno be stopped.[4]

No attention was paid by the Government to any of these representations and protests.

CZAR'S GOVERNMENT MALICIOUSLY SPREADING FALSE CHARGE OF TREASON AGAINST JEWISH PEOPLE—

THE KUZHI MYTH.

A myth was elaborately worked up concerning the engagement near the borough of Kuzhi. The reverses of the Russian troops at that place were blamed by the military authorities upon the Jews, and a skillfully concocted story was circulated for general consumption. Our Messenger, the organ of the staff of the northwestern army, reported in *its* issue of May 5/18: "On the night of April 27-28 (May 10-11) an attack was made by the Germans at Kuzhi, a little to the northwest of Shavli, upon a portion of one of our infantry regiments which was resting. This incident revealed the shocking treachery of a certain element of the local population, especially of the Jews, against our forces. Prior to the

197

arrival of our detachments at this borough the Jews had concealed Germans in many of its cellars and set Kuzhi on fire on all sides at a signal given by a shot. Leaping from the basements, the Germans rushed to the house of the commander of our infantry regiment." etc.

This story, written up in conformity with the accepted rules of the Government's pogrom communications, winds up with the following moral: "This regrettable incident once more confirms the fundamental requirement of field service; the necessity of guarding all important points which had been held by the enemy and are mostly inhabited by Jews."

The Kuzhi incident has been extensively exploited by the authorities for Jew-baiting. Thus even in far off Tashkent, where there are scarcely a score of Jews, notices were posted in the streets on May 7/20 announcing that on the 9th/22d of the month memorial services would be held in the local cathedral in memory of those who had fallen at the borough of Kuzhi, "through the treason of the Jewish population."[5]

Upon investigation made by Deputy Kerensky, of the Imperial Duma, the whole story proved to be a fabrication.

1 Retch. 137, 1915; Haint, No. 123,1915.

2 Retch, May 6, 1915.

3 Jewish Week, No. 2,1915.

4 Russ?????, May 29, 1915.

5 Haint, May 20, June 2,1915.

OFFICIAL GOVERNMENT PUBLICATIONS FALSELY ACCUSING THE JEWISH PEOPLE OF

TREASON.

The official organs of the Government have industriously circulated obviously false stories of alleged treasonable conduct of the Jews.

Thus in the Government Messenger of May 3/16,1915, the following dispatch appears from Kielce: "On April 30/May 13, while the Kossacks were successfully shooting up from an ambush an enemy detachment entering the city, they were witnesses of its reception by a Jewish delegation."

Thus, the Jews were said to have been tendering a reception to the Germans under rifle fire. This self-evident absurdity was transmitted to the foreign press by the Petrograd telegraph agency. The official organ of the war ministry, the Russian Invalid, is especially zealous in accusing the Jews of treason. Here are a few of its outbursts. When nearly a hundred bombs were thrown on *** from German aero planes the official editor, commenting upon this fact, insinuated that the bombardment of a city inhabited by Jews was rather perplexing, since "the German reconnaissance bureau had mostly recruited its agents among them." [1] Later, when the German forces began to press toward Libau, the Russian Invalid said, editorially: "Among the measures for fighting the Germans in the Baltic region we note the expulsion of the Jews from all Kurland, which is carried out with extraordinary energy. Evidence of their guiding the Germans to Shavli has been secured." The absurdity of this item is obvious. The Kurland Jews living north of Shavli are alleged to have "guided" the Germans who were pressing toward the town from the southwest. The fabrications of the Russian Invalid about Jewish war prisoners displayed an extraordinary heinous spirit. The Jewish soldiers are said to be enjoying especial privileges in German prison camps. " The Germans have granted them unlimited power over other Russian prisoners; they are supplied with rubber clubs especially recommended by the German general staff, which they use to beat up their Gentile fellow prisoners who have been found guilty of some transgression. The Jews make extensive use of these plenary powers and even abuse their rights, making sport of the Russian soldiers and instigating the German guards against them, as a result of which torture is frequent." [2]

JEWS BARRED FROM THE GULF OF FINLAND TO BOLSTER OF SUSPICION OF TREASON.

The calumny of Jewish treason is drummed into the heads of the ignorant masses in a. variety of ways. At the approach of the summer season the commander of the Kronstadt fortress issued an order barring the Jews from summer resorts within the zone of fortifications along the coast of the Gulf of Finland. The governor of Vyborg followed suit and gave orders to bar the Jews from country houses in those portions of the Vyborg Province which are within the Kronstadt and Vyborg fortification zones. [3]

JEWISH PRISONERS RETURNING FROM GERMAN DETENTION CAMPS ALSO BARRED.

The military commander of the city of Reval went them one better. He issued an order forbidding entry and residence within the limits of the Reval fortification zone to Russian subjects of Jewish faith returning from German detention camps, where they had been held asprisoners. [4]

JEWISH SOLDIERS ON THE FIRING LINE TREATED AS SUSPECTS.

Notwithstanding the fact that more than 300,000 Jews are fighting along with others on the battlefields, the military authorities are deliberately trying to arouse distrust against the Jewish soldiers among their Gentile comrades. Thus, by order No. 1193 of the general staff, under date of April 27-May 10, 1915, the rank and file were instructed "to watch the Jewish soldiers, whether they readily surrendered as prisoners, and their conduct in general."

1 New Voskhod, Apr. 24-May 7, 1915.

2 Haint, June 10, 1915. Russian Invalid, No. 124, 1915.

3 New Voskhod. 1915. No. 11-12. 14.

4 Retch, June 16/19, 1915.

DISCRIMINATION AGAINST JEWISH WOUNDED SOLDIERS.

The treatment accorded by the Government to Jewish soldiers wounded in battle is illustrated by the following examples:

Early in October, 1914, at a meeting of the Zemstvo Union, in Moscow, a communication was read from one provincial committee to the effect that a wounded Jewish soldier, relieved from further service because of the amputation of his right arm, was about to be expelled to the "pale of Jewish settlement" in western Poland, which was then held by the enemy.[1]

In January, 1915, the minister of the interior made it known that even those Jews who had been in active service in the field during the present war could obtain relief from the laws restricting the residence of Jews only by a special order of the ministry of the interior, in each individual case, upon the petition of the person concerned.[2]

About the same time the following incident occurred: In an engagement with the Germans, Private Rozhkoff, a Jew, lost his left eye. The physicians sent him to Kharkoff to have an artificial eye put in. Upon his arrival at Kharkoff, his passport was stamped "To leave immediately."[3]

In May, 1915, deeming it wise under pressure of public opinion, the minister of the interior, somewhat to relax the rigor of the law toward crippled Jewish soldiers, issued the following order: "Jewish privates who, upon leaving the hospitals, will be admitted for special treatment, to be provided with artificial limbs, to the house of refuge organized by the society for the protection of the health of the Jewish inhabitants, are permitted by the minister of the interior to stay in the capital for a period not to exceed two months, provided that the said persons will be admitted to the said house of refuge upon certificates from physicians in charge of the municipal or military hospitals showing that they are in need of further treatment." [4]

GOVERNMENT JEW-BAITING AIDED BY REACTIONARY PRESS.

The Government is neatly aided by the reactionary press in the circulation of stories of Jewish treachery. Here are a few samples. The Novoye Vremya assured its readers in the mast serious manner that in Russian Poland the Jews transported "hundreds of poods[5] of gold into Germany in coffins. In a letter dated from Warsaw, the story in a certain Polish borough (its name was cautiously withheld) a coffin was opened at a Jewish funeral procession, and. instead of the corpse, there was found in it one and a half million in gold destined for the Germans.

A similar story was told in the Lithuanian anti-Semitic paper. Litvucs Zenlos. No. 182. The Jews were alleged to have dug an underground tunnel from Shavli, through which they drove cattle and poultry into Germany. As the transportation facilities of the tunnel seemed to have been inadequate, a German Zeppelin was said to have descended from time to time at Shavli. where it collected cattle and geese from the subservient Jews and carried this cargo to Prussia.

REACTIONARIES CLAMORING FOR A POGROM.

Not only do the subsidized "Black Hundred" papers clamor about "treason," but they plainly call for pogroms: "See who is thy enemy. For Jews there is no excuse and there must be none. From century to century this tribe, accursed of God, has been hated and scorned: the blood of Russia's sons betrayed by it will long still cry for vengeance."[6]

NO EVIDENCE OF JEWISH TREASON. JEWS TRIED BY COURT-MARTIAL ACQUITTED.

It is worthy of note that the Government, notwithstanding its influence upon the courts, has failed to make out a single case in support of the legend of Jewish treason. Even the courts-martial, notorious by their severity during the punitive expeditions following the Revolution of 1905, have not succeeded in finding even a semblance of proof of

Jewish complicity in military espionage. All attempts of this kind have ended in a fiasco. On March 9-10/22-23, 1915, before the court-martial in Warsaw,

1 Retch, Oct 8/21, 1914

2 New Voskhod, No 5, 1915.

3 Razsvyet No. 5, 1915

4 Razsvyet No. 21, 1915

5 A pood is over 36 pounds avoirdupois

6 Volga, May 8/21, 1915

26106—P—16-3

seven Jews from the boroughs of Groicy and Nowe-Miasto were tried upon the charge of high treason. The charges were found to be so utterly absurd and were so completely refuted by the testimony of the witnesses that upon the motion of the military prosecutor the court dismissed the case against all the defendants.[1]

BLACKMAILERS CONVICTED OF FALSELY ACCUSING INNOCENT JEWS OF TREASON. SEVENTEEN JEWS HANGED UPON BLACKMAILERS INFORMATION.

The way in which cases against Jewish "spies" are manufactured was revealed in Lomza on the trial of officers Chusranyk, Doroshenko, and Mickiewicz, of the reconnaissance detachment, upon the charge of extortion. The evidence against them showed that they had planted a telephone with a Jewish proprietor of a moving-picture show, Eisenbiegel, arrested him on the charge of "maintaining communication with the enemy," and demanded 5,000 rubles of him to set him free. On their trial the fact was brought out that 17 Jews had been hanged upon similar charges, trumped up by Chupranyk. The court sentenced two of the prisoners to six years' imprisonment, while the third one, who turned state's evidence, and disclosed a long series of facts of similar kinds, was allowed to go free. Thus the order to search for telephones had encouraged blackmail and led to the destruction of many innocent Jews.

NEST OF TREASON IN HIGH GOVERNMENT QUARTERS.

Since the beginning of the war there have been convicted of military espionage Col. Myasoyedoff Baron Grotgus, and Fernat, all high officials of the imperial police department. "Treason," said a member of the Duma Kerensky, in a letter to the president of the Duma, "has made its nest in the ministry of the interior."

The reactionary press made an unsuccessful attempt to fasten the blame for Myasoyedoff on the Jews, claiming, as usual, that he himself was a Jew, that his real name was Goldstein, or that he was married to a Jewess, or that his grandmother had been a Jewess, etc. In this way the staging is being prepared for an "outburst of popular wrath," which is to bring death and ruin to the masses of the Jewish people.

VIII. EXILES BROUGHT BACK TO SERVE IN THE ARMY.

45. The following telegram from Vilna, under the date of May 29, 1915, appears in the Russkoye Slovo, No. 1231: "A party of Jews, subject to conscription, and lately deported from Vilkomir, have passed through Poltava on their way back to Vilkomir. They all have been furnished with temporary certificates for admittance to the cities of the province of Kowno."

IX. JEWS PUNISHED FOR SPEAKING THEIR NATIVE LANGUAGE.

46. The petty persecution of the Jews is manifested in the following characteristic fact: " Itsek Levit, 59 years of age, keeper of a bakery shop at No. 85 Sadovaya Street, Petrograd, has been deported to the Province of Yeniserisk (in Siberia) for the period of duration of martial

law, for talking in the German language over the telephone." [2] Two days later in the same Petrograd, for similar offenses the following penalties were imposed upon gentiles: For speaking German over the telephone one, Prashitsky, was placed under arrest for three weeks, the penalty being commuted to a money fine; another, Maryanum, for spreading false rumors and talking in the German language over the telephone, was placed under arrest for one month.[3]

The mere juxtaposition of these facts clearly shows the discrimination against the Jews. Moreover, it is hardly open to doubt that Levit spoke in Yiddish and not in German. After the declaration of war, however, the officials suddenly began to confuse the Yiddish language with the German. The Jews are forbidden to use their native tongue even in private life, as shown by the following fact: " By order of the Petrograd chief of police, dated June 24, Shlyoma Sklovsky, Dveyra Sklovskaya, Nakham Ravich, and Yosif Elyasheff have been sentenced each to a fine of 100 rubles or to arrest for one month for talking in the Yiddish jargon." [4]

1 New Voskhod, No 14, 1915.

2 Retch, June 17, 1915

3 Retch, June 19, 1915

4 Den, June 25, 1915

X. RUSSIAN GENTILE BUSINESS MEN TAKE EXCEPTION TO THE CZAR'S ANTISEMITIC POLICY.

47. The native gentile Russian business men are opposed to militant anti-Semitism of the Government. Its economic interests require, if not complete civic equality of the Jews, at least the repeal of the most outrageous disqualifications imposed upon them, such as the "pale of

settlement," and the percentage restriction of the number of Jewish students admitted to educational institutions (technical in particular). They consider it absolutely necessary for the economic development of the country to grant the Jews freedom of choosing their residence. They have repeatedly given expression to their sentiments during the war at their conventions, viz., at the convention of representatives of finance, commerce, and agriculture, held in April, at the convention of the representatives of gold mining in February, and through their permanent organizations, such as the National Board of Trade and Industry and governing committees of the exchanges in many cities.

Especially characteristic in this respect is the inquiry addressed by the Moscow Merchants' Association to country members, dealers, manufacturers, etc., on the subject of the best means of combating "German economic domination." The replies nave been published as a special report, from which the following is quoted:

"All of the replies favor the abolition of the 'pale of settlement.' This measure is considered * * * primarily as one of the means for combating German influence in our industry. The hope is expressed that the abolition of the pale of settlement' will encourage the activity of the middlemen and introduce them to the great masses of the consumers."
1

APPENDIX.

I. A FEW NEWSPAPER REPORTS OF THE EXPULSION OF THE JEWS.

(a) Poland.

1. During the two days of February 7-8, 1915, 20,000 Jews arrived in Warsaw.[2]

2. As early as January, 1915, 1,000 Jews came to Kielce and 1,500 Jews to Radom from small towns around.[3]

3. In March, 1915, the whole Jewish population, without distinction of

age, position, or wealth, was expelled from certain district of the Provinces of Radom and Kielce,4near the zone of military operations

4. Early in May, 15.000 Jews were deported from the Provinces of Kielce and Radom to the Province of Lublin.[5]

5. In Lomzha there gathered nigh onto 900 exile families. For the most part these are from Yedvabno, who were driven to Lomzha after their expulsion; then again residents of Novgorod and Piontica, a suburb of Lomzha, whence the inhabitants were also expelled.[6]

6. The exiles from Rozhany, Province of Lomzha, 150 families in number, were wallowing in the field in the vicinity of Ostroff, entrance to which was forbidden to them by the police.[7]

7. The New Voskhod of April 17, 1915, reports that the expulsion of Jews from many places in the Province of Suwalki has begun; the next issue of the same paper (April 24) brings detailed data.

In the borough of Merech Province of Grodno. 350 families suddenly arrived last week from the boroughs of the Province of Suwalki. This throng, about 2,000 persons in all are supplied with "certificates of passage," for proceeding into Provinces situated in the Dniepr Basin.

The borough of Yezno. Province of Vilna.is overcrowded with Jews expelled in April from the Province of Suwalki. Boroughs of Seree. Simno. Balwerzizki, Preny, and others. The inhabitants of the borough of Yezno themselves "are full of apprehension for their own fate as well.

Exiles from the Provinces of Suwalki have begun to come to Vilna. All their property has been left by them to fate. They were compelled to leave their homes in the course of a few hours. The first party of 45 persons came from Silen with "passage certificates "for Nadezhdinoand Kaminka in the Province of Yekaterinoslav.

1 The Jewish Week, No 5, 1915

2 Haint, Feb 8, 1915

3 Haint, No's 23 and 24, 1915.

4 Diennik Polski, No 95, 1915

5 Retch, No 127, 1915

6 The Jewish Week, No 2, 1915

7 The Jewish Week, No 1, 1915

Some of these exiles left property worth tens of thousands of roubles at home. The second party from Kozlova-Kuda came under guard.

8. The Razsvyet of May 10,[2] 1915, supplements this picture with new details: "For several weeks now nearly 3,000 exiles from the Province of Suwalki have been in Morech. There is no way to forward them further, owing to the impossibility of obtaining trains. One can imagine in what congestion, under what incredible conditions these 3,000 persons are living in this small borough, without any facilities to shelter so large a number of people.

" In Balwerziszki the Jews, prior to their expulsion, had suffered abuse and humiliation to which even Jews, and even in these times, have not been used." Four hundred families were forced to leave Preny.

9. "On April 14, 1915, a train with 500 exiles passed from Grodno to Vitenbsk. All of them are exiles from the Province of Suwalki, from Lipsk, Kopciowo, Sopockin, Dolynka. Krasnopol, Syen, and others."[1]

10. "The trains with exiles from the Province of Suwalki have moved on with large parties for Vitenbsk (500 people), Mohileff (400), Kremenchug (365), Ooman (200). [8]

11. According to a telegram to the Utro Rossii of June 9, 1915, "special cars have been assigned for the transportation of 20,000 women, expelled from Warsaw, as having no definite occupation."

(6) *Province of Grodno.*

12. As early as in the month of March steps were being taken to expel the Jews from the Province of Grodno. The Razsvyet of March 29, 1915, reported that "in the last few days over 800 families had received official notice ordering them to depart immediately. They succeeded in having their departure postponed until after Passover. "

In Zhitomir a telegram to the following effect was received from the Kieff Jewish aid committee: "The departure of 5,000 women, children, and old folk from Grodno is imminent. Many working women from Shereshefski's tobacco factory are among them." [3]

13. "The first party of exiles, 300 in all, from among those expelled from Grodno, is due in Berdicheff during the next few days." [4]

14. The entire Jewish population is expelled from Druskeniki.[5]

15. By order of the military authorities, the Jewish inhabitants of Knyshin, Goniondz, and vicinity of the Byelostok district of the Province of Grodno, 6,000 persons in number, were ordered to leave within three days, beginning May 4. Subsequently the date of their departure was extended to May 13.[6]

16. The Kiev Oskaya Mysl of May 28, 1915, reports: "Yesterday a party of 600 Jews, deported from Grodno for the time of the war, came to Kieff. The party is made up of women, children, and a small number of old people. The Jews are bound for Yelisavetgrad and Yekaterinoslav."

17. "Homel: 214 exiles have arrived from the Province of Grodno."[7]

(c) *Kurland and Kowno.*

18. Owing to the expulsion of the Jewish population from the Province of Kurland there is a great influx of Jews in Riga, who are on their way to the places assigned to them for temporary residence. They come by railway, on steamboats, in vehicles, and on foot.[8]

19. One thousand Jewish exiles arrived in Orsha from Kurland. Of these 150 were domiciled in the neighboring little towns, the others in Homel.[9]

20. Eight hundred Jews were deported from Kurland to Mohilef .[5]

21. From Mitau the news comes that 8,000 Jews arrived simultaneously in Ryezhitsa. Province of Vitebsk.[5]

22. On May 18, 1915, there were in Riga 9,600 families of exiles, or nearly 42,000 persons, of whom the majority had come from seven districts of the Province of Kurland, and 15,000 persons from the Telshi, Shavli, and Ponyevyezh districts of the Kovno Province.[10]

23. On May 22 a party of 150 exiles from the Province of Kovno came to Byelaya Tserkov.[11]

1Razsvyet. No 18, 1915.

2 Razsvyet, 1915, No. 19.

3 New Voskhod, Apr. 10, 1915

4 New Voskhod, Apr. 24, 1915

5 Razsvyet, May 10, 1915.

6 Retch, 1915. No. 127.

7 Haint, June 5, 1915

8 Retch, May 3,1915.

9 Haint, May 20 1915.

10 Jewish Week, No. 4,1915.

11 Kievskaya Mysl, No. 145, 1915.

24. "Out of the 3,000 exiles from Kovno who had poured into Simferopol, there had been sent to Melitopol 650 persons: To Oryekhoff, 400; to Bolshoy Tokmak, 500; to Berdyansk, 600; to Chernigovka, 100; to Mikhaylovka, 150; to Nogaysk, 150; and to Genichesk,400. In Smorgon, 1,200 exiles from the provinces of Kowno and Kurland have gathered; 107 exiles have arrived in Vilna from Boguslavichi; 350 exiles came also to Vilna from the boroughs of Gelovan, Seym, Ozere, and others. They are being deported to other towns."[1]

25. The expulsion from Kurland overlapped the boundaries of that province; simultaneously with the order of April 30 an order was issued to expel the Jews from the zone of the Ustodvinsk fortress, which includes also the outlying districts of Riga.[2]

26. By order of the Riga military authorities steps were taken to expel again the Jewish exiles who sought refuge along the seashore.[3]

(d) TWO HUNDRED THOUSAND EXPELLED PROM KURLAND AND KOWNO.

27. After the expulsion from the Kurland and Kowno Provinces nearly 200,000
assembled in the Vilna Province alone.[4]

(e) MISCELLANEOUS.

28. The following telegram appeared in the Russkoye Slovo: "To-day, trains are passing filled with Jews expelled from the Kowno region. Altogether 8,000 Jews have passed by to-day."

Vitebsk, May 8: "During the last three days over 20,000 Jews expelled from Kurland, Kowno, and Ponyevyezh have passed through Vitebsk."

29. The Razsvyet, of May 24, 1915, reports:

"Mariupol. Several thousand Jewish exiles have arrived here."

'Poltava. Five hundred Jews, principally from the Province of Kowno, have arrived. They have been lodged in the barracks. Later 1,400 more have arrived."

30. The Jewish Week, No. 3, 1915, gives the following chronicle:

"In Berdyansk, during the last days of May, 920 exiles arrived from the Province of Kowno. The majority of them are old people and children. Some are quite feeble, unable to move without assistance. Many have lost their parents and children on the way. As for property, that goes without saying. The need of medical aid, and chiefly financial aid, is enormous. Clothing and underwear are a necessity,

"In Yelisavetgrad, 1,000 exiles have arrived from the Provinces of Grodno and Kowno.

"Romny. Two hundred Kowno exiles have arrived.

"Toward the end of May 226 exiles arrived in Berdieheff

"Six hundred and five exiles from the Provinces of Plotsk and Lomzha arrived in Kharkoff from Kieff on May 25 and 26.

"Over 100 horse carts with exiles from Shirvinty, Gelvany, and Boguslavishki, principally women, children, and old people, came to Vilna on May 23.

"Bobruysk, A party of exiles. 200 in number, passed through Kieff."

31. "On June 3 horse carts with exiles from Zhosla and Meyshagola arrived in Vilna. From Grodno, 1,200 exiles passed through Vilna en route to the Provinces of Chernigoff and Poltava" [5]

32. "On June 8, 20 conveyances with exiles, principally women, children and old folk, came to Vilna from Shirvinty. Exiles also came from Yanoff and Shaty" [6]

33. The Retch of June 9, 1915, has the following report:

"In the latter part of May a noisy wave of exiles came with a rush. Several thousand people passed daily through Vilna. When the force had subsided, there were found nearly 8,000 stranded on the Vilna shoals -in asylums, houses of refuge—and over 2,000 people in private quarters"

34. The same correspondence states that in the small borough of Shirvinty, Province of Vilna, there have gathered nearly 3,000 exiles.

35. "Trains with exiles have been dispatched to Orsha, Mglin, Kremenchug, Bolotsk, Khorol, Konstantinograd, Mirgorod. In Kishineff a telegram was received on May 10 from the Petrograd Jewish community that no fewer than 400 exiles from the Provinces of Kowno, Kurland, Lomzha, and Grodno were due there." [7]

1 The Jewish Week, No 2. May 31, 1915.

2 Razsvyet, No 19, 1915

3 Jewish Week, No 6. June 28, 1915.

4 The Jewish Week, No. 2, 1915

5 The Jewish Week, No. 4, 1915

6 The Jewish Week, No. 5, 1915

7 The Jewish Week, No. 1, 1915

II. RECORD OF THE RIGA JEWISH AID COMMITTEE.

36. A telling list of telegrams sent by the Riga Jewish Aid Committee to the Moscow Committee appeared in the Jewish Week, No. 3, 1915:

1. On May 24, at 9 p. m., a train with exiles was dispatched: To Romny,

225 persons; to the city of Syeversk 125; to Novozybkovo, 52. Itinerary: Vitebsk-Zhlobin-Homel.

2. On May 25, 53 exiles were dispatched to Lokhvitsa, 70 to Sosnitsa, and 80 to Romny. Itinerary: Vitebsk-Zhlobin-Homel.

3. Beginning with today we are compelled to forward from Riga daily, Fridays and Saturdays not excepted, 1,000 Kurland and Kowno exiles. Postponement has been absolutely denied. On the evening of May 26 a train of exiles was dispatched to Borzna, 200 persons; to Piryatin, 200: to Zolotonosha, 200: to Sosnitsa, 200.

4. To-day, May 25, we have dispatched trains of exiles to Zolotonosha, Piryatin, Borgdn, Mirogod, Kremenchug, 200 each.

5. On May 29, a train with 1,000 exiles was dispatched to Priluki, Piryatin, and Pereyaslav.

6. On May 30, a train with 1,100 exiles was dispatched to Melitopol.

7. On May 31 there have been dispatched 800 exiles to Kremenchug, 400 to Krolyevets, 70 to Konotop.

8. On June 1, 1,000 exiles were sent to Berdyansk,

III. REPORT8 OP THE MOSCOW JEWISH RELIEF SOCIETY.

(a) On the condition of exiles from Poland.

37. An awful picture of the condition of the exiles in Poland is drawn in the reports submitted to the Moscow Jewish Relief Society for War Victims by its delegates, who had made a tour through Poland. This is, e. g., what one of these representatives writes regarding the condition of the Jewish population of the Province of Lomzha:

"It can not be said that it has been ruined, because that word does not make clear the true reality, does not reveal the true scope of this terrible event. In cases of ruin something is preserved at all events, some however wretched remnants, in the extreme case at least the ruined place, at least the old site in ashes. But here the people have been cast out onto a desert road, as if after a shipwreck or an earthquake. Thousands of families, tens of thousands of persons, naked and barefoot in the literal sense, with children in their arms, old and young, looking for shelter and bread, are roaming among the hamlets. The disaster has not spared anybody, has made all equal, and erstwhile wealthy men apply to you for a few pounds of potatoes." [1]

(b) *Expulsion from the Province of Grodno.*

38. The delegate of the Moscow Jewish committee reports from Byelostok, under date of May 30:

"On the 23d instant a train with 650 persons was dispatched to Yelisavetgrad; to-day other trains are to be sent to Berdicheff, Rovno, and Vinnitsa. Expulsion from a part of the Sokolka district of the Province of Grodno has been announced. From Kuznitsa 120 families are to be expelled; from Novy Dvor, 110 families: i. e.. nearly 1,000 persons. The date set is June 3 at the latest." [2]

IV. EXILES BARRED FROM MANY SECTIONS.

39. The territory where the exiles were permitted to seek refuge was restricted by the administration. At first the Dnieper region was designated for them. Then came an order from headquarters forbidding settlement on the right bank of the Dnieper.[3]

The sections where the exiles were permitted to settle soon became overcrowded. The local authorities, on the other hand, in many places denied admittance to the exiles.[4]

Thus the Kieff military district[3] and the Province of Yekaterinoslav[5] were closed to the exiles.

1 The Jewish Week, No2. 1915.

2 Jewish Week, No. 3, June 7, 1915.

3 Jewish Week No. 3. 1915.

4 Minutes of the serial meeting of the Jewish relief committee for war sufferers, held on May 21, 1915 Jewish Week. No. 3, 1915

5Haint No 142, 1915

V . LISTS OF PERSONSLOST BY THEIR FAMILIES APPEARED DAILY IN THE NEWSPAPERS.

40.The following notice, which appeared in the Kievskaya Mysl of May 28, 1915,is quoted as a specimen:

"Forwarding herewith the inclosed list of relatives sought by the Jewish exiles who have arrived in Bakhmut from Kowno and vicinity, we respectfully request you to publish it in the next issue of your esteemed paper. (A long list of names follows.) Signed Committee of the Bakhmut Branch of the Society for the Relief of the Jewish Inhabitants Suffering from the Military Operations."

VI. INSANITY AMONG EXILES.

41. On May 27,1915, there were brought to the Jewish Hospital of Vilna 8 mentally deranged from among the exiles of the Province of Vilna. In the course of three weeks 28 mentally deranged—26 women and 2 men—were registered among theexiles.[1]

VII. SUFFERING OF THE HOMELESS EXILES.

42. According to the report to the Jewish Week from Kiev, Jewish exiles who arrived there on May 19 from Kowno were living together with the women and children in freight cars at the railway station, awaiting to be forwarded to Berdicheff and Byelava Tserkof.[2]

43. "There are at this moment in this city (Vitebsk) over 3,000 exiles, most of them women, children, and old people, incapable of work. The

exiles are sheltered in the synagogue building, without light, in congestion and overcrowding. Many sleep on the floors." [3]

44. A report from Berdyansk states that several hundred exiles from the Province of Kowno have been housed in barns.[3]

1 Jewish Week, No. 3.1913. Vilna Courier, May 29.1915.

2 The Jewish Week No. 2.1915.

3 The Jewish Week, No. 3, 1915.

Grant Gochin is a Litvak who has been researching his family history for the past 30 years. Professionally, he is a certified financial planner and a wealth advisor in Encino, California. He also serves as the Honorary Consul for the Republic of Togo, and as secretary of the Executive Committee of the Los Angeles Consular Corps. Grant is philanthropically, culturally, and socially involved. The Lithuania-related Boards on which he sits are LitvakSIG and Maceva. Grant is married with one son.

FIFTY PERCENT OF THE ROYALTIES FROM THE SALE OF THIS BOOK WILL BE DONATED TO:

The Survivor Mitzvah Project is a 501(c)(3) non-profit public charity dedicated to bringing emergency aid to elderly and forgotten Holocaust survivors in Eastern Europe who are ill and alone, and lacking food, medicine, heat, and shelter.

Made in the USA
San Bernardino, CA
11 April 2019